Gospel Portraits

Gospel Portraits

*Reading Scripture as Participants
in the Mission of God*

K. Rex Butts

WIPF & STOCK · Eugene, Oregon

GOSPEL PORTRAITS
Reading Scripture as Participants in the Mission of God

Copyright © 2022 K. Rex Butts. All rights reserved. Except for brief quotations in critical publications or reviews, no part of this book may be reproduced in any manner without prior written permission from the publisher. Write: Permissions, Wipf and Stock Publishers, 199 W. 8th Ave., Suite 3, Eugene, OR 97401.

Wipf & Stock
An Imprint of Wipf and Stock Publishers
199 W. 8th Ave., Suite 3
Eugene, OR 97401

www.wipfandstock.com

PAPERBACK ISBN: 978-1-6667-3716-5
HARDCOVER ISBN: 978-1-6667-9630-8
EBOOK ISBN: 978-1-6667-9631-5

03/23/22

All scripture quotations, unless otherwise indicated, are taken from the New Revised Standard Version Bible © 1989 Division of Christian Education of the National Council of the Churches of Christ in the United States of America. Used by permission.

Scripture Quotations labeled CEB are taken from the Common English Bible, copyright 2011. Used by permission. All rights reserved.

Scripture quotations marked (KJV) are taken from The Authorized (King James) Version. Rights in the Authorized Version in the United Kingdom are vested in the Crown. Reproduced by permission of the Crown's patentee, Cambridge University Press

Scripture quotations labeled NIV are taken from The Holy Bible, New International Version, NIV®. Copyright © 1973,1978, 1984, 2011 by Biblica, Inc. ® Used by permission. All rights reserved.

Scripture quotations labeled (NJB) are taken from The Holy Bible: The New Jerusalem Bible. Biblical text copyright © 1985 by Darton, Longman, and Todd Ltd. and Doubleday, a division of Random House, Inc.

Scripture quotations makes NLT are taken from the Holy Bible, New Living Translation, copyright © 1996, 2004. Used by permission of Tyndale House Publishers, Inc. Wheaton, Illinois 60189. All rights reserved.

Scripture quotations marked MSG are taken from The Message, copyright © 1993, 2002, 2018 by Eugene H. Peterson. Used by permission of NavPress, represented by Tyndale House Publishers, Inc. All rights reserved.

Dedicated to Laura, my wife,
Who has supported me and loved me in life.

Contents

Acknowledgements | ix
Introduction | xi

Part One: What's Up With the Bible?

1 The Holy Bible: Please Don't Overlook Jesus | 3
2 Hermeneutics: When Reading the Bible Hinders Mission | 15

Part Two: Discipleship and the Church

3 Following Jesus: The Invitation, the Challenge | 33
4 God's Artwork: The Church as the Embodied Gospel | 46
5 The Living Bible: A Library with One Story to Tell | 63

Part Three: A Missional Reading of Scripture

6 Back to the Bible: A Narrative Reading of Scripture | 79
7 Renewing Our Imagination: Entering the Gospel Story as a Church | 96
8 Living Gospel: A Faithful but Contextual Performance of the Story | 107

Part Four: Christ-Formed and Spirit-Filled

9 The Christ-Formed Church: Reclaiming Our Identity as Kingdom Citizens | 119
10 The Spirit-Filled Church: All People Blessed to Bless All People | 129

Conclusion: Think Local, but What If . . . | 145
Bibliography | 151

Acknowledgements

As I'm sure many other authors know, writing a book is a labor of love who has benefited from the help of many others. First and foremost, is the help of my wife, Laura Butts. This book springs from many years of theological education, pastoral ministry, and life experience—some very painful days along the way. Yet Laura has been a constant supporter and encourager. Without her insistence on how she believed God was leading us, I would have neither stepped onto the path of vocational ministry nor completed the theological education I have had the blessing of receiving.

Along with acknowledging my wife, I must acknowledge my children Kenny, who is no longer with us, as well as Caryn and Jared. Through them, I have learned a lot about life and Christian faith, which has undoubtedly had an influence on this book.

I am also appreciative of my friend and former Professor, John Mark Hicks, who was kind enough to read a draft of this book and offer constructive feedback. However, his help with this book began many years ago in a seminary class he taught on theological hermeneutics. In that class, I was able to begin naming the problems I saw with the way I was taught to read the Bible and begin formulating a better hermeneutical lens for reading the Bible.

I am also thankful for David E. Fitch, who directed the Doctor of Ministry cohort in Contextual Theology at Northern Seminary, and Rich Little, who supervised my Thesis. This book is a product of both my studies as a participant in this cohort and the thesis.

Acknowledgements

You've also heard the saying that behind every good author is a good editor and that is certainly true in this case . . . Well, at least the good editor portion. I am thankful to both Frances Story and Sarah Friedline, the office managers of the Newark Church of Christ, who read and helped edit early drafts of this book. Likewise, I am thankful to Miranda Mendoza, a freelance editor who worked really hard to edit, format, and turn this manuscript into the book it is. Along this line, I am also thankful to the staff at Wipf and Stock for taking a chance on me and publishing this book.

Last but not least, I am thankful for the Newark Church of Christ who I have the privilege of serving among as a pastor. Serving as a pastor during the Covid-19 pandemic has come with many challenges and writing a book certainly did not lighten the load but doing so was possible because I am blessed to serve among such a wonderful congregation. This includes the encouragement always received from Richard Duzan, Bennett Foster, and Joe Giubardo, the shepherding elders among our church, as well as our campus minister Casey Coston and our worship/community minister Nicole Da Cunha.

Introduction

I JUST BOUGHT A new Bible to preach from the other day, a *New Revised Standard Version* of the Bible from Oxford University Press. I hate to admit it, but I'm getting older. My eyesight is too, so the Bible I was preaching from was getting difficult to read. I already wear progressive contact lenses, which are supposed to help with both near and far-distance reading. But that help only goes so far, so I bought a new Bible with a slightly larger font. Perhaps now, when preaching, it won't be such a struggle to read the Bible.

We face another challenge today as people who seek to read the Bible, a collection of writings that we regard as sacred writings inspired by God. The contexts in which the various books of the Bible were written are far different from our own, which are far removed by time and distance. While many of the stories and teaching seems understandable, sometimes the difference between then and now creates questions that we may not always have satisfactory answers to. Now, two decades into the twenty-first century, we are faced with other questions that are not always so easy to answer and may even seem impossible to answer. Even if we grant that the Bible answers all of life's biggest questions, we are left to ask how the Bible offers such answers.

The question of how we read the Bible matters as much as whether we read the Bible. It's a question that has to do with the subject of hermeneutics, which has had my attention for years. Perhaps that is because I realized there were problems with the hermeneutic that shaped the way my church

Introduction

tradition, in the Stone-Campbell Restoration Movement, read the Bible. However, participating in *a cappella* Church of Christ, I remember singing the song "Give Me The Bible." The words of the refrain, which read like a prayer, has the church singing . . .

> Give me the Bible—holy message shining,
> Thy light shall guide me in the narrow way.
> Precept and promise, law and love combining,
> 'Til night shall vanish in eternal day.

This hymn recognizes that besides the guidance found within, the Bible speaks in a variety of ways. We know also that the Bible contains different genres. So, reading the Bible is a little more complicated than just opening the pages and doing what we read.

Part of the challenge is that sometimes we come to the Bible with questions for which the Bible has not directly sought to answer. Yet there is a temptation to take an answer from the Bible and, with little discernment, impose this answer as a response to a question the Bible isn't answering. For example, the Bible does not offer any direct answer to the question of Christian unity in a world where many different Christian denominations exist. Likewise, the Bible doesn't have any direct answer to the question of God's judgment upon those who have never had an opportunity to hear of Jesus, and yet this is a question asked by more than a few people. The Bible was written within a framework of a closed universe, and yet we know the universe is most likely expanding. Similarly, the Bible was written in a worldview where belief in God or gods (theism) was unquestioned, whereas we live in a secular age in which such belief is very much questioned and thus formed by a different imagination.[1] Today, understanding how life works must not only take into account religion but also draw from fields such as biology, sociology, and psychology, with discoveries in these fields that were unknown to the writers of scripture. This is not to say that every scientific theory known today is correct or that we should no longer trust the Bible as a reliable guide for what we believe as Christians. I'm simply trying to acknowledge some of the complexity at hand as we seek to read the Bible today.

---

1. Taylor, *A Secular Age*, 368, points out that our present secularized social imaginary is formed by "the market economy, the public sphere, [and] the polity of popular sovereignty . . ."

Introduction

Tomáš Halík, a Catholic priest, philosopher, and theologian from the Czech Republic, has acknowledged this complexity with somewhat of a provocative challenge.

> We are confronted by a whole set of specific questions that did not confront the people of the Bible, and if we substitute our problems for theirs, and relate answers to other questions to our own problems, then it is not the 'Bible itself' that speaks from our words, but instead our all-too-human manipulation of God's world—and such manipulation is unavowed, unthinking, and often simpleminded. Such overuse and abuse of the Bible is irresponsible not only vis-à-vis Scripture, but also toward those with whom we still have sufficient credit for them to invite us to dialogue and a joint quest.[2]

In one sense, I hope this book is an answer to the challenge Halík observes. That is, this book seeks to get us beyond a simple reading that uncritically imposes answers to the problems the writers of scripture were addressing upon the questions we are faced with today. But that is just the start.

The concern of this book is with the church participating in the mission of God and how the Bible shapes the imagination of the local church for such participation. To state the concern as a question: How should a local church read the Bible in order to participate in the mission of God within the local context the church inhabits? This book seeks to answer this question, so what follows is the articulation of a missional hermeneutic.

The book begins by identifying problems that impede church participation in the mission of God. The first chapter, *The Holy Bible: Please Don't Overlook Jesus*, examines ways in which Christians read the Bible but somehow miss Jesus, which is ironic since we are called to follow Jesus. The second chapter, *Hermeneutics: When Reading the Bible Hinders Mission*, addresses some of the changes we are experiencing in America. These changes have helped reveal some of the limitations to the hermeneutical lenses that many Christians wear as they read the Bible, affecting our participation in God's mission.

Following the first two chapters, the book begins laying the foundation for a missional hermeneutic. The third chapter, *Following Jesus: The Invitation, the Challenge*, defines our Christian Faith as one following Jesus. That may sound rather obvious, but in a day when people can claim Christianity as a religion without any commitment to discipleship, it's important to remind ourselves that we are called to follow Jesus because this is the

2. Halík, *Night of the Confessor*, 135.

Introduction

foundation of a missional hermeneutic. The next chapter, *God's Artwork: The Church as the Embodied Story of the Gospel*, turns our attention to ecclesiology or a robust theology of the church. Viewing the mission of God through a Christ-centered and Kingdom-oriented lens, the church understands itself as the instrument by which God carries forth his mission in the world today. So, a missional hermeneutic is ecclesiological in practice. The fifth chapter, *The Living Bible: A Library with One Story to Tell*, encourages us to move beyond reading the Bible merely for knowledge. While knowing what the Bible says is indispensable to reading the Bible well, the aim of a missional hermeneutic is the way we live and whether our lives tell the story within the Bible.

With the next three chapters, we encounter the main aspects of a missional hermeneutic. The sixth chapter, *Back to the Bible: A Narrative Reading of Scripture*, advocates for reading the entire Bible as one story that centers on Jesus Christ and is oriented toward the fulfillment of the kingdom of God. The caveat is that we learn to read the Bible so that we may live as epistles of Christ. This caveat leads us into the seventh chapter, *Renewing Our Imagination: Entering the Gospel Story as a Church*. Here we consider what it means to see ourselves within the biblical story as people who are formed in the way of Christ. By locating ourselves within the story, we are able to hear the truth among a pluralistic society and distinguish the gospel story from other stories. This takes us to chapter eight, *Living Gospel: A Faithful but Contextual Performance of the Story*, which lays out a model for discerning how to live out the gospel story. This model guides the church toward a participation that is coherent with the biblical story but one that is improvised for the context, the particular time and place in which the church is living the story.

The last two chapters of this book were additions to the original vision of this book. The missional hermeneutic this book advocates assumes that the best theological praxis is always locally contextualized. Therefore, rather than telling a church what sort of practices and changes are necessary for continued participation in the mission of God, the local church must engage in such discernment themselves. Nevertheless, I realize that some readers may question how this missional hermeneutic works, how it might reshape the way in which the church embodies the gospel. So, the last two chapters take up this question. Chapter nine, *The Christ-Formed Church: Reclaiming Our Identity as Kingdom Citizens*, describes how this missional hermeneutic opens space for the formation of the church as Christ-formed

Introduction

people. When we understand our formation in Christ within the story of Scripture, we rediscover our distinctive identity as the church and what it means to live out of our identity in Christ. The last chapter, *The Spirit-Filled Church: All People Blessed to Bless All People*, contends that a proper reading of the biblical story means that all believers are blessed by God to live as a blessing to others. This blessing is the reception of the Spirit who is given to all believers without any distinction and the belief that participating in the mission of God means allowing every believer to serve as the Spirit has gifted them—including women who have received the gift of preaching, teaching, and pastoring.

As stated earlier, this book is about learning to read the Bible for participation in the mission of God. The hope is that participation results in an embodiment of the gospel, a dynamic witness that is both faithful to the gospel and contextual to our own times. In other words, my prayer is that this book will help churches live as gospel portraits.

With such a vision, let me offer another caveat about reading the Bible and Christian Faith. Reading our Bible matters, knowing a thing or two about Christian theology, and having some familiarity with church history or Christian tradition will help. Understanding the cultural dynamics of our society will help as well. But none of that matters without the virtue of humility. John Cassian (d. 437) once said, "If you wish to attain to true knowledge of the Scriptures, hasten to acquire first an unshakeable humility of heart. That alone will lead you, not to the knowledge that puffs up, but to that which enlightens, by the perfecting of love."[3]

As you read this book, may it be so with a humility that desires to know nothing other than Christ, the power of his resurrection, and the sharing in his sufferings, that we may become like Christ. We can trust that God is with us, that the Holy Spirit will fill us with the power to live as faithful followers of Jesus contextually participating in the mission of God.

---

3. *Conferences,* 14.10 in Clément, *The Roots of Christian Mysticism,* 101.

Part One

What's Up With the Bible?

1

The Holy Bible

Please Don't Overlook Jesus

> "I like your Christ, I do not like your Christians.
> Your Christians are so unlike your Christ."
>
> —MAHATMA GANDHI

NOT MUCH IN THE news, good or bad, really surprises me anymore, but occasionally there are stories that just baffle me, especially when they involve Christians. Take, for example, the story of Theresa Kenerly, the mayor of Hoschton, Georgia, a small town about fifty miles northeast of Atlanta. She came under fire recently with accusations of racial discrimination when she allegedly excluded a man from consideration for a job "because he is black, and the city isn't ready for this."[1]

In defense of Mayor Kenerly, Councilman Jim Cleveland tipped his own racism, saying, "I'm a Christian and my Christian beliefs are you don't do interracial marriage. That's the way I was brought up and that's the way I believe."[2]

---

1. Joyner, "Georgia mayor under fire for alleged remarks about black job candidate."
2. Edwards, "Georgia councilman says interracial marriage is 'just not the way a Christian is supposed to live.'" Councilman Cleveland added "I have black friends, I hired black people. But when it comes to all this stuff you see on TV, when you see blacks and whites together, it makes my blood boil because that's just not the way a Christian is supposed to live."

Part One: What's Up With the Bible?

In other words, despite the fact that Councilman Cleveland claims to be a Christian, neither the good news of Jesus Christ nor the Bible really matters. That's because his upbringing, rather than his new birth in Christ, is the foundation for his moral authority. So, it really doesn't matter what the Bible says and how the scriptures bear witness to the gospel.

Of course, for many Christians, the Bible is considered *The Authority*. Yet the way many Christians read the Bible seems far removed from the gospel of Jesus Christ. Such is the case of one recent story in *The Washington Post* about Pastor Grayson Fritts of the All Scripture Baptist Church in Knoxville, Tennessee.[3]

Pastor Fritts, who also serves in law enforcement, made the headlines for his sermon condemning gay people whom he referred to as "freaks," "animals," and "sodomites." He said that he was "sick and tired of sodomy being crammed down our throats" as he began his rant. Even more astounding was his claim that the government has the moral authority to enforce Leviticus 20:13, which says, "If a man has sexual intercourse with a man as he would with a woman, the two of them have done something detestable. They must be executed; their blood is on their own heads."

By enforcement, this Pastor meant that civil governments have the moral authority from God to have the police arrest LGBTQ+ people, try them in a court of law, and if found guilty, execute them. Yes, execute them. Put them to death for engaging in homosexual behavior because that is what Leviticus 20:13 says.

At least, that is what Pastor Fritts believes.

Now, like you probably do, I completely disagree with Pastor Fritts. As a follower of Jesus, I believe he is unequivocally wrong. Even more, as a pastor, I find his views very scary and troubling. However, this has nothing to do with what I or anyone else believes about sexual morality. Where Pastor Fritts has gone wrong is the way he is reading the Bible.

Just as I am sure Pastor Fritts believes, I too believe that all Scripture is inspired by God (2 Tim 3:16). In fact, not only do I believe in the inspiration of the Bible, but I also believe the Bible speaks with an authority that has a say in the way we are to live as followers of Jesus. That is, the Bible is the word of God to us, and it is therefore instructive to us as we journey through life participating in the mission of God. So, in addition to

---

3. Chiu, "'They are worthy of death': A cop preached that the government should execute LGBTQ people."

the views he expressed, Pastor Fritts and I disagree on the way we should read the Bible.

Cherry-Picking the Bible

It is rather ironic that in the video clip of Pastor Fritts preaching, he rhetorically asks the question, "How can you cherry-pick one verse, Christian, and say that I don't agree with that one verse because it isn't popular?" And yet, it appears that he has done just that with his use of Leviticus 20:13.

Think about it this way. As followers of Jesus, if we are going to invoke the Levitical Laws of the Torah at face value, then what about the other numerous laws mentioned in Leviticus?

- Shall the civil authorities enforce bathing upon a man whenever he ejaculates (Lev 15:16)?
- Shall the authority require farmers to leave some of their harvest at the edges of the field to feed the poor and immigrants living among society (Lev 19:10)?
- Shall law enforcement enforce a dress code for men that requires growing out the hair of their foreheads and not shaving their beards (Lev 19:27)?
- Should the government execute children who curse their mothers and fathers (Lev 20:9)?
- Should those caught in the act of adultery be executed (Lev 20:10)?
- Should society execute all the mediums—the psychics and fortune-tellers—by stoning (Lev 20:27)?
- Should all forms of work be discontinued on Saturday, the Sabbath (Lev 23:3)?
- Should the government disregard separation between church and state by executing everyone who blasphemes the name of the Lord (Lev 24:16)?
- Should all farming be discontinued every seventh year as a special Sabbath rest (Lev 25:2–4)?
- Should the nation again allow the purchase of people as slaves (Lev 25:44–45)?

Part One: What's Up With the Bible?

Remember, cherry-picking Scripture isn't allowed. So, if someone believes the government should arrest, convict, and execute people for engaging in a homosexual relationship because, at face value, that's what the Bible says, then they must also believe the same for the rest of the Levitical laws too.

But nobody, to my knowledge, really believes this about the Bible, and even if they claim such, they don't practice their belief consistently. I don't personally know Pastor Fritts, but I doubt he believes all of the laws mentioned in the book of Leviticus are still enforceable today, much less by law enforcement.

This sort of biblicism—the kind that says, "The Bible says it, I believe it, that settles it"—is one way of reading the Bible. But as we see, it's a way of reading that cherry-picks the Bible. This happens in a variety of ways that are driven by a variety of "*prebiblical* interests" of those reading the Bible and doing the cherry-picking.[4] That is, everyone opens the Bible with a set of lenses that shapes the way they read the Bible. Nobody opens the Bible as a pure blank slate to take in what the scriptures teach without any interpretation. Our postmodern age has debunked such a modern myth.

So, we are all wearing a set of lenses through which we read the Bible. These lenses mean we have some pre-commitments or pre-biblical interests, good or bad, that shape the way we read Scripture. Therefore, as good as it is that we read the Bible, how we read the Bible matters just as much, if not more.

A question we are faced with as we read the Bible is what kind of pre-commitments we bring. I am a committed follower of Jesus who believes the entire Bible is true. That is, I believe that all of Scripture, the Bible as the Old Testament and New Testament, from Genesis to Revelation, is trustworthy[5] to reveal the will and interaction of God the Father within history that is fulfilled through his Son, Jesus Christ, by the power of his Spirit. Yes, I am Trinitarian in my pre-commitments, and I believe that Scripture faithfully narrates God's plans for all of life, beginning with creation and culminating as a new creation in Jesus Christ.

That also brings up a second pre-commitment: I believe we must learn to read the Bible as a text for following Jesus as we participate in the mission of God. This pre-commitment is why I am writing this book. It seems these

---

4. Smith, *The Bible Made Impossible*, 31.

5. In acknowledging the Bible as trustworthy, I accept the classic definition of infallibility which means that scripture is "not liable to deceive" and therefore the human authors of scripture, guided by the Spirit, will not lead the readers of the Bible astray, see Grenz, *Theology for the Community of God*, 398.

days that there are Christians who read the Bible but are failing to see Jesus or at least see him as clearly as he would like.

A little more than ten years ago, the book *Unchristian* was published, shocking the sensibilities of more than a few Christians. Based on research, the authors explained how the emerging generation perceived Christians as having unchristian characteristics:[6]

- Hypocritical—inauthentic and unreal, conveying a polished image that is inaccurate.
- Too Focused on Gaining Converts—appearing to see people more as targets than people.
- Anti-Homosexual—bigoted people who harbor disdain for LGBTQ+ people.
- Sheltered—too simplistic and out of touch with the realities of a complex world.
- Too Political—motivated by political agendas, typically leaning toward conservative ideologies.
- Judgmental—quick to criticize others, begging the question of whether we really love people as we claim.

You might be thinking, "Well, that's just their perception of Christians," and that is true. But even so, while perception and reality normally differ, there is usually some truth, perhaps a lot of truth, to the perception. How much truth is perception? That's difficult to answer in any case, but in this case, there were more than a few Christians—myself included—who were not surprised at all by the findings.

Years ago, I played in a co-ed softball league, and the team I was on had a significant entourage that always hung out with us during our games. What I remember about this team is that there were a significant number of people on both the team and in the entourage who either identified as LGBTQ+ or had a close friend who did.

I was only one of two people on the team who was a professing Christian, but try imagining the surprise when some of the others realized I was a pastor. It was only a few months later that I began reading the book by Kinnaman and Lyons, which only cemented what I already perceived to be true for a significant number of my fellow Christians. As I listened to the

---

6. Kinnaman and Lyons, *Unchristian*, 29–30.

stories, almost every one of the people that identified as LGBTQ+ grew up attending a church where they encountered hypocrisy, judgmentalism, preaching that seemed driven more by American politics than the gospel, and an often subtle but palatable disdain toward them.

Of concern here isn't anyone's view regarding sexual morality. What we should be concerned with is a posture that doesn't reflect Jesus whom we are called to follow, that doesn't seem to embody the good news of Jesus Christ and the kingdom of God he proclaimed. There are likely more than a few reasons for this, but one of those reasons stems from the way churches have read, or misread, the Bible.

Missing Jesus

The incoherency observed between who Jesus is and who Christians appear to be is a problem. As followers of Jesus, which is who we are called to be if we profess the Christian Faith, we can't quote Jesus' words "I am the way, and the truth, and the life" (John 14:6) as a mere proposition. Jesus wasn't just making a claim about in whom eternal life is found. He was also claiming that his way of life is *the way of life*. In other words, Jesus isn't just a set of truths we must believe; he is a living person but also the Living God in the flesh. The life Jesus lived matters because it is that way of life that he taught us to live so that we would serve as witnesses among the world to the kingdom of God he has inaugurated. Jesus said to his first disciples, "But you will receive power when the Holy Spirit has come upon you; and you will be my witnesses in Jerusalem, in all Judea and Samaria, and to the ends of the earth" (Acts 1:8). I believe this witness that goes to the ends of the earth is still ongoing today as churches embody the gospel. But we won't if we miss Jesus, overlook him, or ignore him.

Reading the Bible is a great blessing and privilege, one that we should never take lightly. The Bible we hold in our hands or have on our smartphones is a Bible that is illegal to possess in some societies. It's also the work for which Christians have given their lives to preserve. So, we are blessed to have a copy of the Bible to read.

As a pastor, I have copies of the Bible in most of the available English translations. In general, I'm thankful that we have access to a variety of translations; there isn't one single translation that's perfect, and anyone who has spent time learning the Bible in its original language (mostly Hebrew and Greek) knows this. It also seems good that there are some good study

The Holy Bible

Bibles available, providing some basic commentary about the historical background and context of the biblical text. The same is true for large print Bibles or Bibles that come with a daily reading plan, as this encourages reading the Bible. However, somewhere along the way, the culture of consumerism has begun to consume the Bible itself.

Have you purchased a Bible for yourself or someone else lately? Not only do you have to decide if you want a large study Bible or something smaller that's easier to carry around, but then you must sift through the different niches of the Bible that are produced for a very specific demographic.

If you're shopping for a teenage girl, there is the *NIV Bible for Teen Girls*. Maybe you're buying a Bible for someone who is very involved in athletics, which means you may want to purchase *The Competitor's Bible: NLT Devotional Bible for Competitors*. Or there is the *NKJV Prophecy Study Bible* if that's your thing. Sometimes, though, it almost seems like the Bible itself isn't good enough anymore and must have some extra dressing applied to sate our own cravings. But the problem with this consumer appetite is it may keep us from seeing Jesus.

Tapping into the resurgence of patriotism, especially among conservative evangelical Christians, one Bible available for purchase is *The American Patriot's Bible* (NKJV):

> THE ONE BIBLE THAT SHOWS HOW 'A LIGHT FROM ABOVE' SHAPED OUR NATION. Never has a version of the Bible targeted the spiritual needs of those who love our country more than *The American Patriot's Bible*. This extremely unique Bible shows how the history of the United States connects the people and events of the Bible to our lives in a modern world. The story of the United States is wonderfully woven into the teachings of the Bible and includes a beautiful full-color family record section, memorable images from our nation's history and hundreds of enlightening articles which complement the New King James Version Bible text.[7]

But if you're just looking at a Bible for men, then how about the *Every Man's Bible* (NIV):

> The Bible for every battle every man faces! This is a man's type of Bible—straight talk about the challenges of life. *Every Man's Bible* has thousands of notes on topics from work, sex, and competition to integrity and more and trusted advice from the pros, just for

---

7. Lee, ed., *The American Patriot's Bible*.

Part One: What's Up With the Bible?

men. *Every Man's Bible* is written by the best-selling author of the Every Man's series, Steve Arterburn.[8]

Or for those seeking a Spirit-filled life, there is the *NKJV Spirit-Filled Life Bible* so that the reader can:

> Encounter the power of the word. Walk in the freedom God intends. Experience the Holy Spirit. For the *NKJV Spirit-Filled Life Bible*, Jack Hayford, founding pastor of The Church on the Way and chancellor of The King's University, assembled a team of respected, Spirit-led scholars to produce this resource of solid biblical truth. Now in a full-color third edition with new contributors, it is even more dynamic. With over 2 million copies sold, the *NKJV Spirit-Filled Life Bible* continues to equip God's people to live in his kingdom, exercise gifts of the spirit, and lay hold of God's promises.[9]

And there's more if none of the above is what someone is looking for.

Here's the problem, though. None of these descriptions mentions a word about Jesus or hardly a word about the kingdom of God—the good news (gospel) Jesus proclaimed. Perhaps it is assumed, but maybe that is a faulty assumption in time where it appears that people can be Christians, even grow up in a local church, but not necessarily be disciples. And yes, that appears to be a real problem today. It's why Michael Frost and Alan Hirsch wrote a book called *ReJesus*, attempting to "reinstate the central role of Jesus in the ongoing spiritual life of the faith and in the life and mission of God's people."[10]

Not only do the descriptions fail to mention a word about Jesus and the kingdom of God, but in editing a Bible by adding material that caters to our various interests, the end-goal for which we are reading the Bible is shifted. When our own consumer interests become the focus of the Bible, our reading of the Bible changes. The change seems subtle, but it is nonetheless significant. The change puts us on a trajectory of reading the Bible with our own life and all of our various interests in mind. Rather than reading the Bible so that we might learn to follow Jesus and in fact become formed in his likeness (Gal 4:19; Rom 8:29), the Bible serves the purpose of

---

8. Arterburn and Merill, eds., *Every Man's Bible NIV*, Deluxe ed.

9. Hayford, ed, *NKJV Spirit-Filled Life Bible*, 3rd ed.

10. Frost and Hirsch, *ReJesus*, 15, who also observed that "a good church upbringing will do many marvelous things for you, but one of the unfortunate things it also does is convince you that Jesus is to be worshiped but not followed" (p. 17).

The Holy Bible

meeting our needs whether it is the need to see how the story of America is woven into the Bible or to get advice from "trusted pros" on life.

No matter how subtle or even unintentional, there is a problem when what draws us to the Bible and what becomes the focus of reading the Bible is something other than Jesus and the kingdom of God. As a pastor, I have seen the problem expressed in the Christian who cherry-picks one Bible verse to justify something that seems so far removed from Jesus that it's comical until it's not.

Several years ago, I was preaching a message on The Sermon on the Mount that Jesus preached in the Gospel of Matthew. This particular message was on Jesus' instruction to love our enemies and pray for those who persecute us (Matt 5:33), whoever those enemies and persecutors may be. As I was preaching, I acknowledged that the ethical questions about participating in war and violence can be a difficult issue. However, I also mentioned that not only does Jesus' instruction seemingly exclude killing our enemies (how can we love anyone we are killing?) but that the life Jesus exemplifies, which reveals the true will of God, is absent of violence toward his enemies. Rather than waging any counterattack against his enemies, Jesus serves by dying on the cross, and that example is the way we are to follow Jesus in living as people who belong to the kingdom of God.

Not surprisingly, a Christian approached me after the sermon to let me know how wrong I was. The individual assumed a hypothetical moral quandary in which another person was being assailed in order to justify violence and killing as morally acceptable. To make his utilitarian argument, in which the end justifies the means, seem "biblical," he reminded me how Jesus told his disciples that they must carry a sword (Luke 20:36). When I pointed out that the reason Jesus told his disciples to carry a sword was to fulfill a prophecy of Jesus being viewed as a criminal (Luke 20:37) and that we still don't have any example of Jesus ever trying to kill his enemies, the response I received was all the more astonishing. This individual insisted that since Jesus is fully divine and the Second Person of the Trinity, that it was Jesus ordering the conquest of violence in the Old Testament book of Joshua.

Astonishing, yes! But not surprising. It's just another example of how Christians cherry-pick Scripture and read the Bible in ways that neglect the story of Jesus and the good news of the kingdom that God is fulfilling in Jesus. More appropriately then, what we have is a misreading of the Bible.

Part One: What's Up With the Bible?

To See Again

Central to the Christian Faith is the conviction that Jesus is both fully human and fully divine. Jesus is the Incarnate Word. God has become flesh (John 1:1, 14), and so we confess that Jesus is the Son of God. The apostle Paul speaks of Jesus as "the image of the invisible God" in whom "all the fullness of God was pleased to dwell" (Col 1:15, 19) or "live in him" (CEB). So, as a matter of faith, the person of Jesus is the fullest revelation of who God is. We know then that it is not so much the case that Jesus is like God but that God is like Jesus. So, it only makes sense that to understand the Bible, we read Scripture in light of Jesus. But doing so requires a new set of eyes.

In the Gospel of Mark, there is a story of Jesus healing a blind man (Mark 8:22–26). The story read in isolation from the context is very strange because at face value, it takes Jesus laying his hands on the blind man twice for his sight to be fully restored. After Jesus initially spits in the man's eyes and lays his hands upon him, the man is able to see but not clearly. The people this man sees look like trees walking around. Although this man now has vision in his eyes, his vision is still distorted and in need of healing—restoration. This healing happens when Jesus places his hands on the man's eyes again.

Now we might ask, why was this man's vision not fully restored the first time Jesus laid his hands upon him. Has something gone wrong with the miraculous power of healing that Jesus has?

Of course, there's nothing wrong with Jesus. The problem is his disciples. Prior to the story of this blind man receiving sight again, the Gospel of Mark tells us about Jesus feeding the four thousand people but more importantly how the disciples still failed to grasp the way in which God is at work in Jesus. It's why Jesus asks his disciples, "Why are you talking about having no bread? Do you still not perceive or understand? Are your hearts hardened?" (Mark 8:17).

Then after the blind man receives his sight again, it will become clear to the disciples that Jesus is the Messiah. But when Jesus begins to talk about his need to suffer the humiliating death of crucifixion and then be raised, his disciples didn't understand. In fact, Peter was so vocal that Jesus had to rebuke him and remind his disciples that they too must deny themselves by carrying their own cross if they want to follow Jesus. However, what Jesus was getting at still didn't register with his disciples. If we keep reading through the Gospel of Mark, we'll see just how much the disciples have yet to understand the way of Jesus as they argue with themselves about who will be the greatest among them (Mark 9:34) and as two of the disciples, James and John, request to sit at the right and left of Jesus in glory (Mark 10:37).

So, what does all of this have to do with the story of the blind man? Well, the disciples are the blind man, and so are we many times. The story of Jesus healing this blind man in two stages symbolizes our own struggle to see clearly who Jesus is and understand the good news of God's kingdom that Jesus proclaimed. The story "invites us to feel Jesus taking us by the hand and leading us to a place where he can enlighten us stage by stage until we see both his own face and the world around us with clarity of vision that mature faith provides."[11] We need Jesus to touch our eyes again and again until we can see clearly what God is doing in Jesus and understand what it means to live as participants in the kingdom of God.

Let me be clear: We need the Bible. We must read the Bible and allow the Spirit to instruct us through Scripture so that we understand the things of God and have the mind of Jesus Christ (1 Cor 2:10ff). Nothing I have said or will say should diminish our need for the Bible. However, we can read Scripture all day long and still misunderstand, still see only people walking around who look like trees. Or worse, we can read the Bible and only see people who need to be killed because they are our enemy or because we've misread the scripture so badly that we believe God has ordained the government to kill such people.

Either way, the problem isn't too much or too little of the Bible. The problem is that we are misreading the Bible. We're misreading the Bible by overlooking Jesus, and in overlooking Jesus, we fail to see who God really is and what he is really doing within history to restore life as a new creation.

Conclusion

We are called to follow Jesus. In the simplest terms, that is what it means to live as a disciple of Jesus. We follow Jesus, learning to live our lives as Jesus lived life, serving and loving people as Jesus did. In doing so, we participate in the mission of God who is at work redeeming his creation.

Whatever participation in the mission of God involves, it will take shape as we read the Bible. But if we overlook Jesus, we'll misread the Bible and then misunderstand what it means to follow Jesus as participants in the mission of God. So, *how* we read the Bible matters as much as reading the Bible, yet we see too many examples of misreading Scripture. What we

11. Byrne, *A Costly Freedom*, 138–39.

Part One: What's Up With the Bible?

need is a new lens or hermeneutic that will allow us to read the Bible in light of Jesus and the kingdom of God. Before getting to this new lens, it will be helpful to see how misreading the Bible has hindered local churches from fully participating in the mission of God, which is where our focus shifts next.

2

Hermeneutics

When Reading the Bible Hinders Mission

> "We have met the enemy and he is us."
> —WALT KELLY

It was very early in the morning for most people but a very late night for my wife and me who spent all night driving from her parent's home in Michigan to our home in Arkansas. As we were driving through the bootheel of Missouri headed along US 412, the highway took a left turn upon entering the little town of Kennett.

As I made the turn, I narrowly avoided a head-on collision with an eighteen-wheeler that would likely have ended our lives, even with our seatbelts on. The collision would have been my fault too, as I realized that I had made a left-hand turn into the right-turning lane for oncoming traffic.

After stopping along the side of the road for a minute to let my heart rate slow down, I was dumbfounded as to how I didn't see that I was turning into a lane for oncoming traffic.

Tired? Perhaps. But I sure didn't seem tired, and I had consumed enough coffee along the drive to feel like I was wide awake. As we continued driving, though, I began noticing that I couldn't read the street signs until I was nearly passing them. The next day, I decided to visit an eye doctor.

Part One: What's Up With the Bible?

As it turned out, my eye exam revealed that I was only able to read the top two lines of the eye chart. The eye doctor told me I needed glasses. Obviously! But alas, I understood why I nearly snuffed the life out of my wife and me by turning into oncoming traffic the night before.

Now as any good preacher knows, there's a sermon illustration here. I thought I could see, and in fact, I saw well enough to fool myself until it almost became deadly when I really just needed better vision. Am I alone? Am I the only person to ignore my poor eyesight? Most likely not, but we'll let that simmer some for now. Meanwhile, as we saw in the last chapter, we need a clear vision to see Jesus and the good news of his kingdom. We need Jesus to touch our eyes again so that we may clearly see him and his kingdom with eyes wide open. But sometimes the problem that keeps the local church from participating in the mission of God isn't just poor vision; it's that we have the wrong script.

Believe it or not, it's entirely possible to read the Bible and entirely miss the point. I once heard a well-intentioned preacher say that he made sure all of his sermons were biblical because he quoted a lot of Scripture every time he preached. Well, I'm sorry to burst the bubble, but quoting Scripture doesn't make a message any more "Christian" than reading the sports section in the newspaper makes me an athlete.

Perhaps we need a reminder that even Satan was quite capable of reciting Scripture, albeit for a sinister purpose. Be that as it may, Christians can misread and misuse Scripture even with the best of intentions.

In a conversation Jesus was having with some of the Jewish people, he said, "You search the scriptures because you think that in them you have eternal life; and it is they that testify on my behalf" (John 5:39). Now I don't doubt that the people Jesus was speaking to believed they were right, but they weren't. Somehow, their reading of the scripture kept them from recognizing the way God was at work in Christ, preventing them from participating in the mission of God.

We're Not in Kansas Anymore

Though churches certainly believe that God is at work in Christ, the way a church reads Scripture may actually obscure this gospel which then becomes a hindrance to mission. The issue is hermeneutical as much as it is missional. Hermeneutics is concerned with the understanding of a text, which involves the skill of interpretation. So, how we read Scripture shapes

Hermeneutics

our understanding of not just a particular biblical text but the Bible as a whole as well as our understanding of God and his redemptive work in history. In turn, how we read Scripture also shapes our understanding of what it means to participate with God in his redemptive mission. Reading Scripture, then, is both a hermeneutical and missional issue or an issue of missional hermeneutics.

Let's be clear on this point. Every one of us and the churches we serve with have a hermeneutic, whether we are aware of it or not, that shapes our understanding of the gospel and the way we then embody the gospel as followers of Jesus. The problem we face is the potential for misreading Scripture and reading the Bible through a hermeneutical lens that hinders mission. To get a better picture of how a misreading of the Bible hinders mission, we need to clarify a few things about our society and the mission that God has called us to embark on as followers of Jesus.

I remember watching *The Wizard of Oz*, the 1939 Metro-Goldwyn-Mayer film, as a child with my siblings and our mother every year. I was always fascinated with the tornado scene because, to the best of my memory, the movie always aired in April, which is the beginning of tornado season in the Midwest.

After the tornado picks up the house that Dorothy is trying to seek shelter in and plops the house down among Munchkinland in the Land of Oz, Dorothy offers the most memorable line from the movie: "Toto, I have a feeling we're not in Kansas anymore."

That's the one line I remember from the movie. But she was right. Munchkinland and the Land of Oz are very different from the midwestern plains of rural Kansas. Like Dorothy, many of us find ourselves living in a very different society than we grew up in. That also means that many of the churches we know and even serve with find themselves dwelling among a society that differs—significantly in many ways—from what existed when those churches were first established. These churches were established among a society that was shaped by the cultural realities of modernism and Christendom. But that was all once upon a time. Society is different now; things are changing and continue to change at such a pace that it's hard to even think about rolling with the changes.

We now find ourselves living among a postmodern and post-Christendom society. As a result of this new reality, the way we live has changed

Part One: What's Up With the Bible?

and will continue changing. The way we live and the structures that people embrace as a society are different from once upon a time.[1]

Perhaps a little reflection on a church I once served with might explain the changes we are experiencing a little more. The church I'm thinking of was embedded within modernism like a fish is to water. There was a sign outside the building which read, "Come, let us reason together." Borrowing a phrase from Isaiah 1:18 in the King James Version, the church had an assumption that others were looking for a church and that coming to faith was a matter of the mind. People just needed to come to the Bible study or worship, to hear the preaching, where the pastor or some other Bible teacher would present a rational lesson.

Of course, we shouldn't be too critical. As much as that church and the many others like them were formed by their understanding of Scripture, they were also shaped by their Americanness too. America, with its "can do" spirit built on the foundation of self-evident truths, was steeped in the Enlightenment thinking that gave us modernism. It was a mindset that is typically traced back to the French philosopher René Descartes, who grounded knowledge in the human mind with his now-famous observation *Cogito, ergo sum* ("I think, therefore I am"). What Descartes meant and what western civilization came to believe was that the human mind, with its capacity to reason, was the foundation of understanding.

Churches established in the late nineteenth and twentieth centuries seemed at home in this modern society. Even with the challenges faced by these churches, it seems like the days that have passed were a much easier time. Many people belonged to a church, and if they moved, they went looking for a new church to join. It was a time when schools and other organizations didn't have activities on Sundays and Wednesday evenings because most people were attending church services then. Also, churches knew how to navigate the waters of the modern and Christendom society they lived among.

Like many churches, Bible study was an important activity at the church of my youth. Knowing the Bible, knowing what the scriptures taught, and knowing the difference between sound doctrine and false doctrine was extremely important. Knowing the truth was a matter of reasoning, deductively putting forth the rational evidence of any claim. And yes,

---

1. This definition is, in my own words, based on Sedmak, *Doing Local Theology*, 74. Sedmak defines culture as "the way we live and at the same time the framework within which we live as social beings." He further describes culture as "multifarious and varies with geographical, social, and historical context . . ."

Hermeneutics

with a bit of hyperbole, a syllogism seemed like the preacher's best friend at times.

The comfort of this bygone era was also made possible by the Church-State culture that the European settlers imported as they forged a new life in America. It's a culture that can be traced back to the conversion of the Roman Emperor Constantine in 312 AD, in which Christianity began to gain favor among the larger society. Eventually, Christianity became the official religion of society, resulting in the Christian church ruling over society as an earthly-Christian kingdom. This became what is now known as Christendom, "which means literally the dominion or sovereignty of the Christian religion."[2] Even though America was founded with a separation between church and state, the reality was that Christianity still wielded much influence over society. As a result, the sort of values and behaviors that were acceptable and even lawful was very influenced by the existence of the Christian church among society.

While many people came to faith in Christ during these years, society was undergoing changes. By the latter half of the twentieth century, modernism and the prevailing Christendom were in decline. For better or worse, the difference we are now facing is so monumental that the best way of describing these changes is to call them a paradigm shift.[3] The new cultural landscape we now live among is postmodernism and post-Christendom.

On the ground, people were asking different questions and even seeking the answers from new sources, even from places that seemed odd for our western culture. This is why the new age section in the religious aisles of your Barnes and Noble grew from a half-shelf to an entire bookshelf or two, maybe even three. It's the same reason why many towns began seeing a new type of business open, usually a little off the beaten path, with a sign that said, "Psychic Readings."

As these cultural changes began emerging, many churches found themselves entering a slow decline, and today that decline is only accelerating. Now there are many other options besides church that became

---

2. Hall, *The End of Christendom and the Future of Christianity*, ix.

3. The concept of a paradigm shift gained attention with the exploration of how scientific paradigms change in the publication of Kuhn, *The Structure of Scientific Revolutions*, 52, who describes a paradigm change as "what fundamental novelties of fact and theory do. Produced inadvertently by a game played under one set of rules, their assimilation requires the elaboration of another set [of rules]. After they have become parts of science, the enterprise, as least of those specialist in whose particular field the novelties lie, is never quite the same."

available on Sundays and even more so on Wednesday evenings. Fishing and golfing, soccer and field hockey, or maybe just staying home to sleep in for one day of the week. At the same time, skepticism is increasing all the more as many of the big "life" answers people previously accepted now appear somewhat, if not completely, inadequate. Another way of saying this is that the maps people once used to navigate life are no longer helpful, as the cultural topography has changed.[4]

Before we get any further, we need to understand something about Christianity and the way we relate to society as local churches. The gospel we have received is universal in scope, but the way churches have often packaged this gospel, bundled within modernism and Christendom, seems incapable of answering the big questions many people are asking. If the story of Jesus is really a gospel of peace, why is there so much violence in the world? And why are Christians sometimes some of the most violent people in the world, clinging to their guns and eager to defend such violence? Or if the story of Jesus is really a gospel that brings reconciliation, why is racism in America still an issue? Why are churches some of the most racially segregated communities around? Why did many churches go silent during the Civil Rights Moment of the 1960s, just like they sometimes still do today as America is still dealing with injustices rooted in racism?

All that is to say: Church, we're not in Kansas anymore! In many ways, it seems like a tornado has picked our churches up from the comforts of a society we became too comfortable in, and now that tornado has plopped our churches down in a strange new place. We can call this place the new post-Christian society we live in. And maybe that's not such a bad thing either—not if we see it as an opportunity from God to reimagine the new ways our churches might continue participating in the mission of God.

The Church and the Mission of God

While some lament these changes and seem determined to navigate their way back, that is a mistake. Never mind the fact that there isn't any going back, longing for the days gone by ignores the opportunity that God is

---

4. Kuhn, *The Structure of Scientific Revolutions*, 109, describes a paradigm as providing scientist with a map as well as "the directions essential for map-making." Then he goes on to make the crucial point that "when paradigms change, there are usually significant shifts in the criteria determining the legitimacy both of problems and of proposed solutions."

Hermeneutics

giving us as local churches. By opportunity, I mean learning how to live as churches on mission with God in some new ways.

Of course, this is easier said than done. One of the challenges means taking an honest look in the mirror and discerning how our churches are embedded in the rural plains of Kansas, while after every Sunday worship gathering, we head back into Munchkinland. But one of the most significant hurdles to overcome is perhaps some of the ways we have learned to read the Bible.

Perhaps getting a grasp on this challenge requires a little more understanding of what the mission of God is and what it is not. I was a seminary student when I first heard about the Christian Doctrine of *Missio Dei*, which is Latin for the "Mission of God." In short, to speak about the mission of God, then, is to say not only that God has a mission but that the mission is an attribute of God. In other words, just as an orthodox faith understands God as all-powerful and all-loving, God is also a missionary or a missional God. Because we also believe that the Bible is God's word, Scripture divulges the fulfillment of God's mission within history.

The problem here is that we haven't always thought of mission as the mission of God. The word *mission* itself is not a new word or concept. Most churches have some sort of missions ministry, perhaps led by a missions deacon or a missions committee, and this often involves the supporting and sending of missionaries to serve among foreign countries.

There's nothing wrong, per se, with such a ministry. However, there was an unfortunate consequence in that many Christians and the churches they served with came to regard mission as just one among many other church activities that typically happened in a foreign context. But *Missio Dei* is much bigger. When we speak of the "mission of God," we are talking about the grand plan of salvation that God the Father, Son, and Spirit undertake within history. Mission is not just another activity of the church; it is the purpose—the very reason—for which the church exists, the singular activity of the church. This is why we can say that it's not the church that has a mission but God who has the church to serve as participants in his mission.[5]

Put another way, this new understanding of the mission means that the church of Jesus Christ, universally and locally, is called to participate

---

5. Wright, *The Mission of God: Unlocking The Bible's Grand Narrative*, 62, "the mission of God is the prior reality out of which flows any mission that we get involved in. Or, as has been nicely put, it is not so much the case that God has a mission for his church in the world but that God has a church for his mission in the world. Mission was not made for the church, the church was made for mission—God's mission."

Part One: What's Up With the Bible?

in the mission of God. And by now, you probably have picked up on that some already. Our participation means we serve as missionaries sent from God the Father into the world as witnesses of his redemptive work in the Son, Jesus Christ, by the power of the Spirit. Now, as fascinating as this may sound, it's also challenging. When we send missionaries to serve in foreign countries, we have learned to think about engaging in cross-cultural missions. That is, the missionaries know they are entering into a different culture, and while they want to faithfully proclaim the gospel, they must do so in a contextual manner.

So, when in Rome, do as the Romans do. Or like the time my wife and I were in Brazil, my wife learned to express the human fellowship we had with other Brazilians by graciously receiving their hospitality. That meant receiving a cup of coffee after dinner with thanksgiving and drinking every last drop even though my wife is not a coffee drinker. Not at all. Period. And she hasn't had a drink of coffee since then, but as a new visitor in a culture different from her own, she didn't want to offend or do anything that might create an unnecessary barrier to Jesus.

What my wife and I both knew was that mission work is about faithfully embodying an indigenous gospel as we tell people about Jesus rather than exporting our American Christianity. Maybe that sounds simple to grasp, but think about that from the perspective of churches, established in a modern Christian society but now residing in an emerging postmodern and post-Christendom culture that is certainly not Christian by any stretch of the imagination. The difference isn't geographical; it is social. But this new social reality requires a cross-cultural approach if churches are to continue any meaningful participation in the mission of God.

How does a local church serve as cross-cultural participants in the mission of God? It's a good question to ask, one for which simple and easy answers will not do. But for churches that regard the Bible as the inspired and authoritative word of God, a significant part of the challenge has to do with how the Bible is read. In fact, every Christian and local church reads the Bible, but *how* they read the Bible is another matter. It matters because the way a church reads the Bible does shape—opening space for or hindering—participation in the mission of God.

Hermeneutics

Could Reading the Bible Hinder?

One of my high school English teachers offered our class extra credit if we would go listen to this evangelist preach at the local civic auditorium. Being the less-than-studious person I was in high school, I needed all the extra credit I could get, and this seemed like an easy way of getting some of that credit. So, I went.

Now, as someone who grew up in church, attending services with my parents whenever the doors of our church building were open, I already had a good basic knowledge of the Bible. I knew enough to know that what I heard that night wasn't the gospel proclaimed by Jesus and his apostles in Scripture. Yes, the evangelist quoted plenty of Scripture, cherry-picking a passage from here and there to bolster his message as being biblical, but what he was selling was what is sometimes called the prosperity gospel or the "health and wealth" gospel.

I'm not trying to malign those believers who claim to have seen or experienced a miracle of some sort. But this was different because this evangelist was promising the people that God was waiting to cure them of every malady if they would just come and receive prayer, all while also telling the people that God was speaking to him directly. And that message was apparently a promise of God's abundant blessing of riches if they would bless God themselves, which apparently meant financially blessing this evangelist who already seemed to have plenty of health and wealth.

This so-called gospel is big business, as it's provided funding for everything from an amusement park to leer jets and big fancy houses, all while seemingly ignoring the mercy and justice for the poor that Jesus cared so deeply for. This story illustrates one way of reading the Bible that has an end very different from the good news of God's kingdom that Jesus pursued. Because the end or goal differs from that which Jesus sought, it actually keeps those seeking such prosperity from participating in this mission of God.

The aim, or *telos*, for which we read Scripture is important. If our reading of the Bible is not shaped by the aim of the gospel, the mission of God, then our reading will take us off track from participating in the mission of God. This seems to happen when the gospel is understood primarily as what Scot McKnight refers to as the *soterian* gospel, which is prevalent among evangelicals who often "equate the word *gospel* with the word *salvation*."[6]

---

6. McKnight, *The King Jesus Gospel*, 29.

Part One: What's Up With the Bible?

We often hear this soterian gospel expressed through the question of "What must I do to be saved?" and "Do you have a personal relationship with Jesus?" Questions like these seem more than appropriate when we read the Bible through the so-called Four Spiritual Laws in which 1) God loves you and created you to live a wonderful life 2) because all people are sinners and are separated from God 3) apart from Jesus Christ who is God's only provision for our sin through whom we can have our sins forgiven and restore a right relationship with God if 4) we place our faith in Jesus Christ as Savior to receive the gift of salvation and know God's plan for our lives. And those who do want this salvation are then invited to pray the "sinner's prayer," which ironically isn't found in any of the conversion stories in Acts, but I digress.

The problem with this way of reading Scripture is that it actually reduces both the picture of the gospel and the promise of salvation that we find in Scripture. In the Gospel of Mark, Jesus begins his ministry by proclaiming the gospel as having appeared saying, "The kingdom of God has come near. Repent and believe the good news" (Mark 1:15, NIV). We will look at this more later, but for now, we must notice that the gospel has something to do with God's kingdom, kingship, or reign. That means that gospel and salvation are something bigger than the emphasis on personal salvation that the soterian gospel has led us to believe.

One of the big problems with the soterian gospel reading of the Bible is that the end, for which is personal salvation, seems to make discipleship secondary or even an afterthought as though it is optional. Though unintended as it is, a person can pray the prayer for salvation and/or be baptized but not necessarily be committed to following Jesus as his disciple. Pastors know this because they know the "frozen chosen" who say they've been saved but in whose lives there is very little, if any, notable difference between them and the rest of the world. Yet if our reading of Scripture can support that we are born-again Christians without a commitment to living as a follower of Jesus, our hermeneutical lens is not only bad, but we are failing to truly participate in the mission of God.

Sometimes, though, Christians can have the utmost desire to follow Jesus and live in obedience to God but still find themselves hindered from participation in God's mission. My own church tradition, the Churches of Christ, are one such example. I don't say this as an insult because they are the "tribe" through whom God has formed me as a follower of Jesus.

Hermeneutics

Many of Churches of Christ were taught to read Scripture and particularly the New Testament as a new law that prescribed the precise pattern for every local church regarding worship and polity.[7] So, the vision of restoring New Testament Christianity assumed the existence of a pattern for the ancient church within Scripture. This required a reading of Scripture, particularly the New Testament, that viewed the New Covenant as a law. Over the years, this approach was solidified and reinforced with slogans such as "no creed but the Bible" and "speak where the Bible speaks and be silent where the Bible is silent." All that was needed was knowing, in short, that God's will for the church was given through direct commands, approved examples, and necessary inferences.[8]

This tripartite method, sometimes referred to in the shorthand as CENI, turned the New Testament into a blueprint for being the church that was read much like one reads an instruction manual for assembling a product. In short, if the local church does everything like it is in the New Testament, then they will be the true church found in the Bible. However, determining just what is a *direct* command, an *approved* example, or a *necessary* inference always seemed as confusing as it was helpful. It did, however, have the effect of turning the Churches of Christ's understanding of the New Testament into an unwritten creed.[9] The result was a fellowship of homogenous churches that historically mirrored each other as though each church was nearly a carbon copy of another.

An unfortunate result has been that in believing there is an ecclesiological pattern in Scripture that must be maintained, missional participation is constricted. Any faithful yet contextual participation in the mission of God among the new post-Christian society is hindered by the belief that the church must restore first-century "New Testament" Christianity.

---

7. So the New Testament from Acts 2 forward became what can be called the canon within the canon. As Campbell, *The Christian System* 157, described the matter saying, "These laws and usages of the Apostles must be learned from what the Apostles published to the world, after the ascension and coronation of the King, as they are recorded in the Acts of the Apostles and Epistles . . . Neither are the statues and laws of the Christian kingdom to be sought for in the Jewish scriptures, nor antecedent to the day of Pentecost; except so far as our Lord himself, during his life time, propounded the doctrine of his reign." Campbell's father, Thomas Campbell, who also was very influential in the early restoration movement described the New Testament as "perfect a constitution for the worship, discipline, and government of the New Testament Church . . .", see Thomas Campbell, *Declaration and Address of the Christian Association of Washington* (1809).

8. Olbricht, "Hermeneutics in the Churches of Christ," 14–15.

9. Hughes, *Reviving the Ancient Faith*, 58.

Part One: What's Up With the Bible?

Onward We Go

Remembering that the mission belongs to God, we know that as followers of Jesus, we are filled with the Holy Spirit to participate in God's mission. The keyword is *participate* or participation, which is something more than just occupying a building in the suburbs and certainly different than standing on a street corner and obnoxiously preaching to passersby.

Answering the question of participating in the mission of God begins, as it should, with God. God is a *missionary God,* and the missionary that he is has sent his Son, Jesus Christ. As we observed in the previous chapter, Jesus is "the image of the invisible God" in whom "all the fullness of God was pleased to dwell" (Col 1:15, 19). So, in one sense, Jesus fully reveals to us who God is, but in another sense, it is God the Father revealing himself through the Son in what we call incarnation. That is, God becomes flesh, becoming fully human in the person of Jesus the Messiah.

The fourth Gospel begins by telling us about this revelation of God by saying, "In the beginning was the Word, and the Word was with God, and the Word was God" (John 1:1). Identifying Jesus as this eternally existent Word, the Gospel goes on to declare that "The Word became flesh and lived among us . . ." (John 1:14). The language here is tabernacle language that speaks of God "dwelling" among us just as he once dwelled among Israel in the tabernacle.[10] The difference is that where God's dwelling in the tabernacle was by means of the Ark of the Covenant, God is now dwelling among us as one of us. God has become a living, flesh and blood human being just like us in Jesus.

Here is where our Christian doctrine of the Incarnation gives shape to our understanding of the mission of God. In the pursuit of redemption, God has come to us and become one of us. Or as the late Eugene Peterson put it in his translation, John 1:14 says, "The Word became flesh and blood, and moved into the neighborhood" (MSG). God did not expect us to come to him and become like him in order to be redeemed. Instead, we are able to come to God and become like God or be made new in the likeness of Christ because God has first come to us and become one of us in the person of Jesus.

So, God undertakes his mission as an incarnational mission, and that becomes the template for how churches participate in the mission of God. This is why those being sent to foreign countries as missionaries receive

---

10. The word used in here is *skēnoō* and is typically rendered as having "made his dwelling" (NIV), "dwelt" (ESV), or "lived" (NRSV) which claims that God took up "residency" in the Word that has become flesh, see Bruce, *The Gospel of John*, 40.

Hermeneutics

training in cross-cultural missions so that their work will be incarnational. That is, in going to serve as a missionary in a foreign country, the missionaries seek to faithfully proclaim the gospel but do so in an incarnational manner so that they are not importing their own cultural expressions with the gospel they proclaim. But what about the local church?

With the emergence of a rapidly changing American society, how does our understanding of incarnational mission shape our participation in the mission of God? Or to ask the question another way, how does a local church shaped by the mindset of a modern and Christendom culture serve as incarnational participants in the mission of God among a post-Christendom culture now shaped by postmodernism?

Besides the cross-cultural challenge of serving in a different social culture, we must also realize that the local culture will vary from place to place. Whatever similarities every American community shares, the differences cannot be overlooked. Memphis, Tennessee, is different from Rochester, Minnesota, which is as different from Boulder, Colorado, as Newark, New Jersey, is different from Newark, Delaware. And now that we are beginning to recognize that America is a mission field,[11] we must think about how the local church must serve as cross-cultural or incarnational missionary communities. Yet the hermeneutical lens through which the Bible is so often read is a hindrance to such participation.

Though I didn't fully recognize it at the time, I've seen how a bad reading of Scripture can severely cripple any participation in the mission of God. When I was a seminary student in Memphis, I began serving with a local church as an associate minister. The church gathered on Sundays in a building located off of Summer Avenue. This was a part of town that had seen its better days pass, which was apparent to anyone taking a quick drive around the neighborhood. Homelessness, drugs, and prostitution on the streets, along with deteriorating homes, spoke loudly of the problems that existed.

The congregation had a sanctuary that could easily seat five hundred people, perhaps even six or seven hundred. And in fact, there was a time when nearly that many people gathered in this sanctuary on Sundays to worship God. But not anymore. Now, there were about seventy-five to eighty or so worshipers, all white and all aging in years.

On most Sundays, the sermons that were preached were very predictable to anyone familiar with the traditional and conservative spectrum of Churches of Christ. The messages focused on a number of doctrinal issues,

---

11. Guder, et al., *Missional Church*, 2.

defending the distinctive views that set apart this church from other denominations, reminding the worshipers how the Bible predicted that many would turn away from "sound doctrine" to suit their own desires (cf. 2 Tim 4:3). But few words were ever spoken about God's concern for the poor. Instead, the poor were viewed as a problem, a threat to the safety of the church members. In fact, a few of the members were so filled with racism and a disdain for all those "homeless bums hooked on drugs," as I recall one man saying, that it made perfect sense as to why this dying congregation was all white.

While there were many reasons behind the slow decline of this once vibrant church, one reason was their misreading of the Bible. The way the Bible was read and preached made minor issues, such as how a church sings during worship, into major issues while failing to see the issues of injustice right under their noses. The way in which the Bible was read, coupled with some implicit (and sometimes explicit) racism and contempt for the poor hindered them from having any capacity for reimagining how God was working in the neighborhood and how they might participate in that aspect of God's mission.

Fifteen years later, I've not forgotten. It's a vivid reminder of just how much a misreading of Scripture can obscure the mission of God, even blind us from seeing how God is presently at work around us and how he is calling us to join him in that work.

Conclusion

I'm not interested in jettisoning the Bible in the least bit, but I do believe that we must learn to read the Bible differently. I seek to follow Jesus, though that sometimes is more of a stumble than a steady walk. However, I'm convinced that faithfully following Jesus, a theme we'll take up in the next chapter, means we cannot simply continue reading the Bible as a text about us, as a text merely about our getting saved, or as some kind of legal text prescribing a monolithic church practice.[12]

---

12. Bosch, *Transforming Mission*, 181, notes the cultural differences as the reason why restoring the past will not work as well as the sort of response such cultural changes requires: "The profound dissimilarities between then and now imply that it will not do to appeal in a direct manner to the words of the biblical authors and apply what they said on a one-to-one basis to our own situation. We should, rather, with creative but responsible freedom, prolong the logic of the ministry of Jesus and the early church in an imaginative and creative way to our own time and context."

Hermeneutics

    I'm thankful for my heritage in the Stone-Campbell Restoration Movement and particularly among the Churches of Christ, which has contributed to the perspective I bring to the text as I read Scripture. That's a perspective shaped by the even larger Protestant Reformation, which sees the need for continued reforming. I see that need too, but I'm still learning.

    During our worship gatherings at the church I now serve, we sometimes sing the song "Simple Gospel," which talks about laying down our religion and other untruths for the simple gospel of knowing and rejoicing in the Lord. That's dangerous if it involves the arrogance of thinking we can simply forget the past and reinvent the wheel, so to speak. But if it means rediscovering how we can participate in the mission of God as a church following Jesus, then by the grace of God manifested in the power of the Holy Spirit, let's do it.

Part Two

Discipleship and the Church

3

Following Jesus

The Invitation, the Challenge

"When Christ calls a man, he bids him come and die."
—DIETRICH BONHOEFFER

IF YOU WOULD HAVE told me twenty-five years ago that I was destined to go study theology and become a pastor, I would have laughed, to say the least. The idea had never even crossed my mind. When I turned twenty-one, I did what many twenty-one-year-olds do—bars and clubs, partying, and living life according to what I thought was a good life.

But I did grow up in church, and while I didn't really know the scriptures, I knew enough to know real Christianity when I saw it. And that is what happened. Among a small church in South Bend, Indiana, I found some Christians who seemed to take Jesus seriously. They not only talked about Jesus, but they were striving to demonstrate who Jesus was in the way they lived. This is when I decided to start following Jesus, and twenty-five years or so later, from that decision, God has led me to where I am now—a pastor.

My number-one job as a pastor is following Jesus, and it would still be my number-one job even if I wasn't a "clergy" person, as society often categorizes my vocation. Your number-one job is following Jesus too, whether you are a pastor or not. If you believe in Jesus, confessing Him as the Son of God who has been crucified, resurrected, and exalted as Lord and Messiah, then you are called to follow Jesus. There isn't any exception. Discipleship is not just an idea that some believers might choose to pursue after coming to faith. Our calling is to follow Jesus, and this is exactly what Jesus expects of us.

For those of us who serve in some capacity of church leadership, it's impossible to lead others in following Jesus if we're not striving to live as disciples ourselves. In fact, in the economy of God's kingdom, to truly be a leader—a pastor, church elder, or even a children's Bible class teacher—is to follow Jesus. Among churches, leaders are followers of Jesus first. But living as a follower of Jesus is never so easy, and Jesus never said it would be. It's never a straight path. Sometimes we take five steps forward only to seemingly fall six steps backward. Other times, we think our life is going well, only to discover it's not. Discipleship is an invitation from Jesus to follow him, but it's also a challenge that will be tested by different circumstances in life, sometimes of our own doing, and sometimes not. Sin, foolish decisions, the lack of discernment, and the complacency of faith coupled with the brokenness of life we all will encounter, make this invitation of following Jesus a challenge too.

With that said, I'm thankful for the grace of God that enables us to keep following Jesus even in the struggles and stumbles along the way. So yes, the steadfast love of God is full of mercy. If it was not, doom would become us all. But at some point, we have to ask introspectively why following Jesus is so difficult. I mean, existentially, we know discipleship isn't easy, but the challenges we encounter should never become excuses that absolve us from taking responsibility. At the end of the day, we either take seriously the invitation and challenge of following Jesus or we don't.

Struggling and Stumbling

When churches offer a general confession of sin during their public worship gatherings, the liturgy of the confession usually goes something like, "Most merciful God, we confess that we have sinned against you in thought, word, and deed, by what we have done, and by what we have left undone." Sin isn't just what we do, but sometimes it's what we don't do. In ethics, this is called the sin of commission (what we do) and the sin of omission (what we do not do). Just because we don't commit robbery, adultery, or some other wicked deed does not mean we don't sin. Maybe our sin was being too busy to help participate in a food drive that will benefit victims of a natural disaster. Or maybe the sin is avoiding a person who is homeless that visits your church occasionally because their life, with all of the problems, is just too much of an inconvenience.

There are numerous reasons we struggle to follow Jesus. Maybe we just don't take it seriously enough. In his book *By The Way*, Derek Vreeland writes, "I realized that even though I had been baptized, I hadn't committed my way to the Lord. I hadn't yet taken my baptismal identity seriously. I hadn't become an intentional follower of Jesus."[1] I could say the same about myself too, as I'm sure many other Christians could as well.

In fact, rather than just confessing other people's sins, I'll share a confession of my own.

Several years ago, I was on my way to a meeting, another one of those pastoral job requirements. I was running a little late, so I had a heightened sense of urgency. Normally, I'm very punctual with time and very task-oriented. So, I'm very zoned in on what I need to do, as I was on this particular day. As I was heading out to my car, I heard my neighbor Rochelle say something. I looked up, smiling toward her as she, this single mother of four children, was sitting in her minivan. I assumed Rochelle was just saying hello. But notice that I assumed. I never heard what she actually said as I returned a polite but quick "I'm in a hurry and don't have the time right now" hello to her.

But then Rochelle said, "Pastor, I could use some prayers. I've been diagnosed with stage-3 breast cancer."

That did catch my attention long enough for me to say, "I'm sorry, I'll be sure to pray for you," before I continued getting into my car. As I sat down in the driver's seat and started my car, it dawned on me that this is not how Jesus would likely respond. So, I quickly got out of my car and walked over to Rochelle's van as she was rolling up the window.

As I approached Rochelle, I looked at her and said, "I'm sorry. You look scared, and you don't just need someone to pray with you later; you look like you need some prayers now."

So, I reached out my hand and, taking hold of Rochelle's hand, prayed for her right then and there. As it turned out, the meeting wasn't that important after all. But God opened space that allowed my wife and me to begin getting to know Rochelle more. That, in turn, opened space for extending more of God's mercy as our church was able to help Rochelle through some of the financial struggles that come with the cost of fighting cancer. And eventually, after surgery and both chemotherapy and radiation

---

1. Vreeland, *By The Way*, 27.

treatments, Rochelle received the gift of healing from God that she needed as her cancer was declared in remission.

Whenever I recall this story, I am reminded of how easy it is to miss the mark in living as a follower of Jesus. It's not because of any evil act or apathy toward discipleship; rather, it's just a failure to act (the sin of omission) because of some bad learned habits. Although we are Christians and seem to prioritize "going to church," we miss the point too often. We're not called to be good church-goers who gather in a building to sing a few songs, hear a word preached from the Bible, and receive the Eucharist. We're called to follow Jesus.

Now please don't misunderstand me. I love gathering with the church in worship and believe there are significant theological reasons for doing so. But just as worship without the practice of justice and mercy is rebuked by the prophets (Amos 5:24; Mic 6:6–8), so it seems that we should rebuke the notion of worshiping and "going to church" without a commitment of living as followers of Jesus.

Christianity, Then and Now

The struggle to follow Jesus isn't just a lack of taking our calling seriously or from persisting in bad habits; sometimes, it's sheer blindness. We've already seen how spiritually poor eyesight obscures our vision of Jesus, causing us to misread the Bible and fail to see how the scriptures point to Jesus. Yet in another sense, churches can suffer from sheer blindness too.

Christianity in the west, especially among churches shaped by white culture, is so accustomed to the Christendom lens that they have become used to the poor eyesight this lens has created. In fact, for many, explaining the Christendom culture is somewhat like trying to explain water to a fish. We are so immersed in the Christendom culture that we don't even know it and have little capacity to imagine any life beyond the aquatic tank of Christendom our churches are swimming in.

This reality of Christendom and the malady it is to our gospel vision is what Lee C. Camp describes as the "Constantinian cataract," which is named so after the Roman Emperor Constantine. After his conversion to Christianity in 312 AD, Christianity became favorable among society and eventually became the official state religion. While this new reality certainly alleviated many hardships and sufferings that followers of Jesus faced throughout the first three centuries, some of the changes were not for the better. Christianity became aligned with the power of the state, and eventually, the bonds of this marriage were so strong that the difference between the two became so blurred that they blended into one. In fact, the church-state began employing the power of the sword to baptize the rest of society into her Christendom way. Christian history is, regrettably, full of examples of Christians killing their enemies in the name of Christ and/or in service to the state. Salvation became less and less about a life that has been transformed by following Jesus and participating in his now-present kingdom, becoming instead about going to heaven (and not to hell).[2]

In this Christendom society, we've come to a point in history where salvation is by "faith alone" even though that phrase never appears in Scripture. Following Jesus effectively became optional for Christians, with the exception of clergy, and today even those who serve as clergy can do so without necessarily following Jesus. Saving faith is seemingly reduced to intellectual assent to the truth of Jesus, leading to a personal relationship with Jesus and perhaps a few new moral behaviors. But then again, I've been serving in ministry for twenty years now, and though all Christians still sin, including me, there are too many Christians whose beliefs, values, and behaviors mimic the rest of society. I've encountered Christians who were not only adulterers but found a way to justify their adultery, while others were greedy and selfish people whose favorite three persons were "me, myself, and I."

Sadly, most Christians have heard of or experienced the pain inflicted by Christians who are egotistic, abusive, misogynistic, racist, and a lot more. I once had a Christian walk out of a worship gathering during a sermon I was preaching, saying that he would never attend a church with a Muslim-loving preacher. As if that wasn't bad enough, later that day, several church leaders tried defending this man by rationalizing his action rather than asking what kind of gospel this man had heard that would allow him to believe such hatred for Muslims is okay.

Among the Churches of Christ, we have historically practiced believer's baptism, and this practice has very much been a part of our identity. Those who confess their faith in Jesus are summoned to be baptized immediately. So, years ago, I was talking with a church about serving as their minister. During a conversation, the church leaders inquired about my understanding of baptism. This didn't come as any surprise, but what was surprising was how quick these Christians were to condemn anyone to hell

2. Camp, *Mere Discipleship*, 22.

that didn't share their view of baptism, yet they were perfectly okay with the fact that two men in their church were racists and purported members of the local Klu Klux Klan.

Not surprisingly, I notified the church that I was no longer interested in serving with them as a pastor. But my intention here is simply to illustrate just how often we have reduced the Christian Faith to a life that reflects very little of the Jesus we read about in Scripture and even learn about from Christian tradition. This explains why there are more than a few books, from the popular to the more academic, addressing the subject of church and discipleship from a variety of angles.[3] Yet what is even more astonishing is that too often, any talk of obedience with saving grace and faith is met with accusations of works-oriented salvation. This is beyond absurd, to say the least. If the apostle Paul can acknowledge being set apart for the gospel in order to "bring about the obedience of faith . . ." (Rom 1:5; 16:26) while writing about the grace of God in Romans, of all letters, then our Christian Faith should do no less.

To speak of faith as obedience or even as allegiance to Jesus[4] is to recognize that we are called to follow Jesus. This call of discipleship became lost in the Christendom marriage of church and state. It's reflected individually among people who profess to be Christian but whose lives pretty much mirror the values of society, particularly a sub-culture within society.

This lack of discipleship has worked itself out among the church, rendering many local churches incapable of participating with God in bringing about the kingdom—heaven on earth. Just consider these words from the late Dr. Martin Luther King Jr.:

> There was a time when the church was very powerful. It was during that period when the early Christians rejoiced when they were deemed worthy to suffer for what they believed. In those days the church was not merely a thermometer that recorded the ideas and principles of popular opinion; it was a thermostat that transformed the mores of society . . .

---

3. Some of these books include most recently Vreeland, *By The Way*; Palmer, *Unarmed Empire*; Bates, *Salvation By Allegiance Alone*. See also Chan, *Multiply*; Breen and Cockram, *Building A Discipling Culture*; Platt, *Radical*; McKnight, *One Life*; Frost and Hirsch, *ReJesus*; Camp, *Mere Discipleship*; Bonhoeffer, *Discipleship*.

4. Bates, *Salvation By Allegiance Alone*, 77, "The gospel reaches its zenith with Jesus's installation and sovereign rule as the Christ, the king. As such, *faith* is Jesus is best described as *allegiance* to his as king."

> Things are different now. The contemporary church is often a weak, ineffectual voice with an uncertain sound. It is so often the arch-supporter of the status quo. Far from being disturbed by the presence of the church, the power structure of the average community is consoled by the church's silent and often vocal sanction of things as they are.[5]

Dr. King contrasts so well the difference between pre-Constantinian Christianity and what has become Christendom Christianity. But what changed from a theological standpoint was the call to discipleship. Writing from a jail cell to justify himself and the movement he was leading, he was having to explain himself to pastors and other Christians whose faith, lacking in a commitment to following Jesus, rendered the church inept to exist as nothing more than a servant of the state upholding the oppressive policies of the state.

This is the way in which Christendom has blurred our vision. Reading the Bible through Constantinian cataracts has muffled—if not completely silenced, in some cases—the invitation and challenge of following Jesus. Whatever status the church has within society, the church is called to serve King Jesus. While the gospel we proclaim is a word of grace to sinners, a word of hope to those who suffer, and a word of comfort to those who mourn, the church is called to be neither a coach nor a cheerleader. Every local church is called to follow Jesus, living as an embodiment of the gospel that Jesus proclaimed, and so participate in the mission of God. We must let go of the Christendom paradigm through which we have learned to read the Bible so that we can read Scripture for the purpose of learning to follow Jesus. Though this will likely be a difficult task, adopting a missional hermeneutic begins with hearing the call of Jesus once again.

"Come, Follow Me . . ."

The Gospel according to Mark opens with these words: "The beginning of the good news of Jesus Christ, the Son of God" (Mark 1:1). The good news or gospel, according to Mark, is about Jesus. It's not about church or salvation, though both church and salvation will come as a result of this good news about Jesus. Mark wants to turn our eyes upon Jesus, to focus our attention on what Jesus will say and do.

---

5. King, Jr., "Letter From Birmingham City Jail," 290.

Part Two: Discipleship and the Church

As Mark tells us about this good news, he introduces us to the message Jesus proclaimed. Jesus enters the region of Galilee, saying, "The time is fulfilled, and the kingdom of God has come near; repent and believe in the good news" (Mark 1:15). He then immediately issues a summons, "Follow me and I will make you fish for people" (Mark 1:17). It's important that we not miss what Mark is telling us about Jesus because hearing Jesus' proclamation and summons is where discipleship begins.

Jesus is literally telling us that the kingdom of God has appeared. No, certainly not in the fullest sense, but the reign of God is coming into existence in Jesus. While the precise nature of the kingdom of God remains open for discussion, a simple way of understanding the meaning of "kingdom" is the sovereignty of God, with his will being done on earth as it is done in heaven (cf. Ps 145:11–13; Matt 6:10).[6] Jesus will fulfill the will of God here on earth as it is done in heaven. But—and this is a big *but*—Jesus also calls us to follow him in bringing about the kingdom of God upon the earth.

This summons is an invitation to come behind Jesus and learn from him how to live this kingdom life, embodying this gospel. In some sense, this invitation is offering us an apprenticeship to become disciples of Jesus, so we follow him to learn from him much like an apprentice learns the building trade from a master carpenter. It's a journey on which we learn to do little kingdom activities well before taking on the bigger. It's sort of like when I started working for my dad, who ran his own excavating business. I told him that I wanted to learn how to run a bulldozer and backhoe. So, my dad said, "Yep!" as he grinned and handed me a shovel, telling me that I would learn how to do all that by learning how to shovel first. I wasn't amused then, but I understand now. As we begin following Jesus, we start out as beginners, but as we continue following, every aspect of our life undergoes a transformation that redefines and reshapes us as Jesus envisions in his own life and teaching.[7]

Following Jesus will challenge us, and there isn't any reason to pretend it won't. One of my favorite Jesus stories occurs at the end of Mark's first chapter where we read about Jesus healing a man with leprosy. In the story, this leprous man doesn't question the ability of Jesus to heal him; he just questions his willingness (cf. Mark 1:40). My hunch is that this man, in the miserable and helpless condition he was, had encountered plenty of religious folks that simply turned away in their unwillingness to help. But

---

6. Ladd, *A Theology of the New Testament*, 60–61.
7. Frost and Hirsch, *The Shaping of Things to Come*, 255.

Following Jesus

Jesus was different. He reached out his hand and touched the man as he healed him.

It's a touching story, no pun intended. I don't know what you believe about Jesus, but I believe Jesus could have healed him from a comfortable and safe distance. But he didn't. Instead, Jesus risked becoming unclean himself and catching leprosy to heal this man by affirming his humanity with a human touch.

I love this story. That was until I was in the city of Belo Horizonte, Brazil, and entered an apartment that was overrun with squalor. I was there at the invitation of a young Brazilian man who was tagging along with the group I was with. Adelfio was his name, and after becoming friends over a couple of weeks, he asked me and several others to come to visit his mother, Eva. This was important to Adelfio not only because he loved his mother and wanted her to meet his new friends but because Eva was disabled after suffering a couple of strokes. My hunch was that Eva likely didn't have many visitors. But as I entered the apartment, I was immediately hit with a nauseating smell of urine and poor sewage, among other smells. But I toughed it out and gladly met Adelfio's mother, which I knew was the right thing to do.

After spending a little time talking with Adelfio's mother, we were ready to leave. The Brazilians that I had met loved to hug as a way of saying goodbye, and Eva wasn't any different. I don't usually have any objections to hugging other people, as it's kind of an unofficial prerequisite of becoming a pastor. But I knew that the smell of urine was coming from Eva, and immediately a reflex was triggered in me. Silently, I was worried about the unsanitary conditions and the possibility of catching any kind of disease or infection. That sounds silly now, but these are the sorts of thoughts that raced through my mind as I was quickly trying to think of a way out of hugging Eva.

It is funny how God works and the way he sometimes speaks to us. Almost immediately as I began thinking about the condition of Eva and justifying why I shouldn't hug her, this story of Jesus healing the leprous man in Mark 1 came to mind. You may call that a coincidence, but I don't. I believe it was the Holy Spirit attempting to remind me that I am called to follow Jesus, reminding me of how Jesus once treated another individual who was regarded as unclean and untouchable. Here was an opportunity to learn what it means to follow Jesus, to live as Jesus lived and love people just as Jesus loved people. But was I up for the task? The Spirit was challenging me as to whether I was going to take following Jesus seriously at this moment by hugging Eva, thereby dignifying her humanity just as Jesus did for this man with leprosy.

And in case you're wondering, I did hug Eva that day and didn't get sick or experience any other adverse result. Instead, Eva smiled as she faintly said, "Deus te ama" ("God loves you" in Portuguese).

The point is that we are called to follow Jesus, and this is what Jesus expects of us. Living as a disciple won't always be easy or convenient. In fact, if we read on in the Gospel of Mark, Jesus eventually begins telling his disciples that he is going to suffer death on a Roman Cross, which was a shameful spectacle that was beyond the imagination of his followers. They were looking for God's promised Messiah and believed that Jesus was this anointed person sent from God, but crucifixion was inconceivable. Except it wasn't for Jesus. To clarify himself, Jesus spoke plainly about what following him meant. According to Mark 8:34–35, Jesus said to his disciples, "All who want to come after me must say no to themselves, take up their cross, and follow me. All who want to save their lives will lose them. But all who lose their lives because of me and because of the good news will save them."

Jim Elliot and his wife, Elizabeth, were one of five missionary couples who went to Ecuador with the intention of teaching Jesus to the Huaorani people, an indigenous tribe. Their story was told in the 2005 film *End of the Spear*. The title of the film hints at the fate of Jim Elliot and four others, Ed McCully, Roger Youderian, Pete Fleming, and Nate Saint.

In a journal entry, Jim Elliot wrote, "He is no fool who gives what he cannot keep to gain that which he cannot lose." He based his reflection on Jesus' promise in Mark 8:35 about how those who lose their lives for his sake will save their lives. This is one of my favorite quotes because Jim Elliot not only lived by the words of Jesus but because they remind me that if we truly believe in Jesus, we have nothing to lose and everything to gain in following him. While most of us will likely never face any sort of persecution and harm for following Jesus, we know that this invitation is challenging too. Nevertheless, Jesus expects us to follow him.

Following Jesus isn't an option. If we want to partner with God in his redemptive mission of bringing about a new creation, we must begin with this simple but significant recognition: We are called to follow Jesus!

Following Jesus

Letting Go

When I was a seminary student, I took a course on the Gospel of Mark. This is where I first began to wrestle with just how serious Jesus is about discipleship. The summons of following Jesus came with a call to repentance and faith (Mark 1:15). We are called to make changes, which is what repentance is about, and believe in the good news of God's coming kingdom that Jesus is proclaiming.

For most of my life, the word *repentance* was associated with turning away from sin, which is part of the textbook understanding of repentance. The sins attached to this association were the "big" sins—immoral behaviors like getting drunk, premarital sex, looking at porn, lying, and cheating. In other words, as a young boy, following Jesus meant no more going out and partying, getting drunk, or getting funny in the backseat of the car. I'm not saying this is wrong. I certainly believe Jesus is calling us to flee immoral behaviors. But as I read through the Gospel of Mark and the other three canonical Gospels, along with the rest of Scripture, there sure seems to be much more to repentance and hence, more when it comes to believing the good news of God's kingdom.

Jesus is calling us to follow him, to come after him and learn from him how to embody this kingdom. That requires a change in the way we live, but since our ways of living are shaped by what we believe and the way we think, what we believe and how we understand what God is doing in Christ must also change. The repentance Jesus calls us to embrace "involves a decision to change one's mind about God and the work of God. It involves new understanding and the ability and willingness to act upon this new understanding. Repentance means to turn away from the old understanding about God and to embrace the new understanding."[8]

Repentance here becomes more of a process than an event. Yes, there is a beginning point, but this is not a one-and-done deal. Changing our minds is a gradual paradigm shift in which we come to believe as Jesus believes about God's work, reign, and mission, embracing the beliefs, values, and practices that Jesus embodies in his life of ushering in the kingdom of God.

This same call of repentance and belief is later issued by the apostle Peter as he preached on the Day of Pentecost in the second chapter of Acts. There Peter was addressing devout Jews who simply misunderstood how the hope their prophets spoke of would be fulfilled. It was unimaginable

---

8. Peace, *Conversion in the New Testament*, 251.

that the promise of salvation that Israel hoped for would come as a result of this Jesus of Nazareth being crucified. Yet this is exactly what Peter proclaimed, letting them know that God had raised Jesus from death and exalted him as Lord and Messiah. But what can they do? Well, they can repent, says Peter. In the passage, Peter says, "Repent and be baptized, every one of you, in the name of Jesus Christ for the forgiveness of your sins. And you will receive the gift of the Holy Spirit. The promise is for you and your children and for all who are far off—for all whom the Lord our God will call." (Acts 2:38–39, NIV).

Just as Jesus himself summoned people to change their expectations of God's work, so also did the apostle Peter. God is reestablishing his kingdom-reign in Jesus whom God has crowned as King. Israel must change their minds and learn to embody the way of life Jesus lived, being baptized in the name of Jesus if they wish to participate in the future of God's reign. But we too must hear this call to repentance and faith.

Criticizing Christianity in America is rather easy these days. Examples abound, some of which have already been mentioned in previous chapters, many of which are low-hanging fruit made easy for the pickings. The problem seems to be a misunderstanding of the gospel and how that gospel lays a claim upon our lives that calls us to follow Jesus, repenting and believing the good news in the way we embody the gospel. This misunderstanding has led to what the late Dallas Willard described as a "gospel of sin management." That is a reduction of the gospel to nothing more than getting saved as an individual or (usually among more progressive Christians) the removal of systematic injustices.[9]

This gospel of sin management is something we must repent of if we are to truly participate in the mission of God. Our understanding of the gospel must open space for following Jesus into the fullness of the kingdom of God that Jesus has inaugurated. Herein is the way in which the local church is formed as a visible sign of God at work in the world.[10] Such a transformation not only requires a different reading of Scripture but will induce a paradigm shift that results in a new way of reading Scripture.

---

9. Willard, *The Divine Conspiracy*, 41.

10. Sider, *The Scandal of the Evangelical Conscience*, 63, "Only if we recover Jesus's gospel of the kingdom and allow its power to so transform our sinful selves that our Christian congregations (always imperfect to be sure) become visible holy signs of the dawning kingdom will we be faithful to Jesus. Only then will our evangelistic words recover integrity and power."

Conclusion

Jesus calls us to come and follow him, leaving behind our old life as we repent and believe the good news of the kingdom of God, so we can live as followers of Jesus. This is the way we as individuals are gathered into local church communities participating in the mission of God.

If only it was as easy as it is to write about it. It's not, and I don't want to pretend like following Jesus is always an easy endeavor. Letting go of the old life, with all of its trappings, is difficult enough. But life also takes many unexpected twists and turns, some of which are full of grief and pain. Few people make it through life without any injuries, and they have the scars to commemorate those difficult moments. I like to remind college students that they probably have yet to live the best part of their lives (at least I hope so) but that they also probably have yet to endure the worst part of their lives too.

These moments of suffering make the already challenging task of following Jesus even more testing, and sometimes we will fall down along the way. So, we are ever thankful for the grace of God that sustains us and allows us to get back up and on track. As we do so, we continue following Jesus, and God becomes not only the center of our lives but the fullness of our lives through the Holy Spirit. As that happens, we become partners with God in the real restoration movement which is living as a new creation in Christ bringing about heaven here on earth—the kingdom of God.

4

God's Artwork

The Church as the Embodied Gospel

"Painting is poetry that is seen rather than felt, and
poetry is painting that is felt rather than seen."

—LEONARDO DA VINCI

THE FIRST ROCK CONCERT I ever saw was the band AC/DC on the *Razor's Edge World Tour* in Chicago, on January 25, 1991, at the Rosemont Horizon arena. I was in high school then, playing the guitar and enthralled with anyone who could play a loud and mean-sounding guitar with just enough bluesy overtones to sound as if the notes were coming straight from the heart. And they were. Watching Angus Young play was mesmerizing, to say the least. As a guitarist, if I could hop in a time machine and transport myself back in time, the first stop would be at the old Filmore East venue in New York City to watch Jimi Hendrix play. Then, on my way back to the present, I would make a stop in Austin, Texas, to watch Stevie Ray Vaughan jam.

But that's mostly the extent of my art. I'm not an actor. I'm not exactly sure what the difference between good and bad photography is—though anything awful is rather obvious. More astonishing to some is the fact that up until a few years ago, I had never visited an art museum. I never had any plans to do so because I never thought it would be something I'd enjoy. That all changed when I was living near Washington, D.C., where thanks to

American tax dollars, admission into the Smithsonian museums is free. So, my family and I visited the Smithsonian American Art Museum.

Wow!

I was more than fascinated to walk through all the galleries and see all of the exhibits. The only problem was that having young children with us, who have limited attention spans, meant that I couldn't stay as long as I really wanted to. Nevertheless, I was captivated. When we left, I wanted to come back for another visit. The beauty and creativity were astonishing in many ways—ways that words can't diligently describe. I wanted to know more about the artists whose works I was seeing. To say the least, my assumptions about what I thought visiting an art museum would be was vanquished. That day, I understood why art was not only aesthetically appealing but how good art had the ability to inspire and even provoke new ways of thinking and being among those who behold what their eyes and ears see and hear. And while I am not even in the same caliber of guitarists as the likes of Jimi Hendrix, Stevie Ray Vaughan, and Angus Young, their playing arouses a desire in me to pick up my own guitar and play—with the volume and gain cranked up.

The Church, Called to Follow

Jesus calls us to come and follow him, so we do so. But this call is never to simply be a bunch of individuals learning to participate in the kingdom of God. The invitation of Jesus is to become a community of disciples who together will live as witnesses of Jesus, people proclaiming the good news of Jesus and the kingdom of God. What we have is an invitation to become the church, but this invitation is a challenge too. As much as I value gathering with my church for worship and fellowship, following Jesus as a church is so much more than "going to church" on Sunday and perhaps a few other occasions throughout the week. Our calling is about a particular way of life so that we embody the gospel in our life that we proclaim as the truth.

This embodied life we live as the church flows from the heart of our character as a church, an *ethos* infused with the gospel and cultivated by the Spirit through, among other things, our reading of Scripture. What should emerge is a gospel culture that offers what can be described as a new social imagination.[1] This new social imagination means we begin understanding

---

1. Mills, *The Sociological Imagination*, 7, coined the term "sociological imagination" to described how people relate the intersecting understanding of what is happening in

Part Two: Discipleship and the Church

our own identity as a church—a new creation in Christ—that is living by a different set of beliefs, values, and habits from that of the world we live among. As we do, the world around us begins to see an alternative way of life that is beautiful, invigorating, and generative of a flourishing life.

It's sort of a cliché question, but if our churches were to disappear today, would it matter to the communities we live in? My answer is yes and no. If every church closed, society would notice, and there are certainly some people who would suffer as a result. There are too many good programs such as food pantries and clothing closets as well as family counseling centers, support groups, and addiction recovery ministries that all provide invaluable services to Christians and non-Christians—often at little to no cost to the person. Surely such people would suffer without the churches that support these programs and ministries.

That being said, the lack of discipleship that has severely weakened our Christian witness means that, at some level, little would be different if our churches were to close. Discipleship is more than just value voting or using social media to call out a select number of injustices so that we appear to be standing on the right side of history. To live as a church embodying the gospel as followers of Jesus is wholly other than being a conservative or liberal, as those cultural philosophies are commonly understood in the current American political binary system. From a gospel perspective, it can be argued that the political binary of conservatives and liberals is just two different sides of the same coin that rejects the kingdom-reign of God. That is, both sides ideally seek freedom as an inalienable right, a concept expressed well by Immanuel Kant.[2] So many Christians living in America embrace an understanding of freedom as their individual and autonomous liberty so long as it does not violate the freedom of others. But this is not discipleship, as it makes this concept of freedom the object of our human desire rather than submitting our will to the Lordship of Jesus Christ.[3] In

---

the world with what is happing in their own lives. By describing the local church as depicting a gospel culture as the new social imagination, I am speaking of believers whose understanding of the world (worldview) and their own individual lives as intersecting with the gospel and having their social-imagination (re)formed by the gospel.

2. Kant, *The Metaphysics of Ethics*, who defined freedom as "the alone unoriginated [sic] birthright of man, and belongs to him by force of his humanity; and is independence on the will and co-action of every other in so far as this consists with every other person's freedom."

3. The Western-Kantinian concept of freedom seeks the removal of any object that hinders the good(s) of human desire and in doing so makes this idea of freedom itself the object of human desire, Highfield, *God, Freedom, & Human Dignity*, 103–4.

essence, it is a continuance of the original sin in which, like Adam and Eve, the individual seeks to become his or her own arbitrator of what is right and wrong. Whereas the truth that Jesus offers, which truly sets us free, is the liberating power of a life lived once again under the heavenly rule of God rather than the self-made tyranny of our own rule.

This is all the more reason we need a new way of reading the Bible. The scriptures we read as the word of God have the power within them for giving us a new social imagination lived under the reign of King Jesus and aligned with the mission of God if we can read the Bible as instruction in following Jesus. Such a hermeneutic opens space for an ancient but fresh participation in the mission of God as followers of Jesus who are faithfully but contextually embodying the gospel as local churches in our local communities. With a commitment to following Jesus, understanding how this reading of Scripture opens the door for an ancient but fresh embodiment of the gospel requires us to go deeper into Scripture.

And the Church Is . . .

In my own church tradition, most local congregations will identify themselves as something like the Eastside Church of Christ or the Main Street Church of Christ. If those names seem lacking in a little pizazz, that's because they do. I'm not trying to be critical in admitting that. The name on the church sign for most Churches of Christ served two purposes. First, the name referred to the local location of the church building, such as a church located on the east side of town or the church on Main Street. But more importantly, the name was about identity. The Churches of Christ ideally wanted others to know that this church was simply a community of believers who belonged to Jesus Christ.

While it may make sense to have a little more attractive or attention-grabbing name on the church sign, the issue of identity cannot be underestimated. Identity is about who we are or who we believe ourselves to be. What we believe about ourselves shapes how we live. This is why in sports, it is so important for the head coach, or manager in baseball, to create a team identity that will translate into a winning culture. That's exactly what former Chicago Cubs manager Joe Maddon did when he told the 2016 Cubs to "embrace the target." As a franchise, the Cubs entered the 2016 season as the favorites to win the World Series, even though they had not played in a World Series since 1945 and had not won the coveted championship since

Part Two: Discipleship and the Church

1908. Yet by telling the players to embrace the target, Maddon cultivated a culture in which the players saw themselves as winners rather than the "lovable losers" that had characterized many previous Cubs teams.

Identity matters in business, in sports, at home, and in a lot of other aspects of life, and it matters most for the church. Who a church is shapes how that church will live. But the true identity of any church is not wrapped up in a creed or any historical movements. As important as the history of local churches are, with their written or unwritten creeds and the historical events from which they emerged, such as the Cane Ridge Revival or the Azusa Street Revival, an identity rooted in Christ as participants in the mission of God is cultivated in following Jesus.

In the previous chapter, we explored what it means to follow Jesus, but we must push farther to understand the identity that Jesus seeks to cultivate in our churches as we follow him. When Jesus began his ministry and calling people to follow him, he did so by proclaiming the gospel. This was the pronouncement that God was restoring his kingdom-reign upon the earth. Some of those followers thought they understood what this meant. That probably holds true for Christians today, but just as the first disciples were in for a surprise, so too might we find ourselves surprised if we follow along with Jesus.

As the Gospel According to Mark tells the story of Jesus, a pattern unfolds as Jesus pushes deeper into what following him and participating in his kingdom really means. In the eighth chapter, Jesus begins teaching his disciples that he must suffer death at the hands of the authorities and then be raised from death (8:31). Peter, the ever brazen leader he was becoming, showed his misunderstanding of what the kingdom of God was really about when he began correcting Jesus (8:32). Jesus immediately called Peter out as an adversary, saying, "Get behind me, Satan." After rebuking Peter, Jesus turned to the rest of his disciples, who presumably shared Peter's displeasure with Jesus, and to the crowd to correct them all. Those who want to follow Jesus into the kingdom of God must deny themselves and embrace the cross, with a willingness to lose their life with Jesus and suffer his shame (8:34ff). Through the cross on which Jesus will be crucified is the only way in which the kingdom of God comes.

But as followers of Jesus, understanding how this path to the kingdom will reform our social imaginations for embodying the gospel may remain elusive. It did for the disciples as Mark tells the story. In the ninth chapter, Jesus again began talking about the necessity of his crucifixion and resurrection (9:31). Yet the disciples again showed their failure to understand when they began arguing with each other about who was the greatest among them. So, Jesus again corrected their misunderstanding, saying, "Whoever wants to be first must be the least of all and the servant of all" (9:35, CEB)—as he welcomed a child and said that this is what it means to welcome him. The lesson is clear: Rather than pursuing our own greatness, becoming a self-sacrificial servant who will welcome even the most insignificant of people, such as a little child, is the only way to keep following Jesus into the kingdom he is inaugurating.

Yet hearing or reading such teaching and understanding is still a challenge. In the tenth chapter of Mark's Gospel, Jesus repeats his warning about what will happen to him when he finally enters the city of Jerusalem. There he will suffer a humiliating and agonizing death, but after three days, he will be raised (10:33–34). Apparently, the disciples still believed that Jesus was on his way to restore the kingdom of God, as two of the disciples, James and John, asked to sit at the right and left side of Jesus (10:35–37). The problem was that they didn't understand what this really meant, and Jesus knew so. He says to them, "You don't know what you're asking. Are you able to drink the cup that I drink, or be baptized with the baptism that I am baptized with?" (10:38).

"We are able," said the disciples as they responded with confidence (10:37), but can they really? Can we?

Can we really drink the cup Jesus drinks and receive the baptism he receives? That's a question we should not be so quick to answer. The question is about embracing the good news of Jesus and the kingdom of God on the terms of God's will. It is about embracing the way of the cross as self-sacrificial servants who are willing to give up all power and suffer while trusting that God will not only vindicate us but will also bring about his promised salvation only through this way of the cross which is the way of Jesus Christ. And of course, we know by faith that God will because not only was Jesus crucified on what we now call *Good Friday*, but then three days later was the first *Easter* or *Resurrection Sunday* when God raised Jesus from death. God then exalted Jesus as the Lord and Messiah, as Jesus ascended to the throne.

Undoubtedly, in the past and even presently around the world, there are people for whom the decision to follow Jesus means facing persecution, even to the point of death. While followers of Jesus do not face such persecution in America, that does not mean that embracing the way of the cross as the way of Jesus is optional. If our desire is to follow Jesus and participate in the mission of God, then we are at a non-negotiable moment of decision. Either we embrace this gospel as Jesus embraces it or we don't. But assuming that is what we desire to do, then we have to begin thinking about what it means and how we read the Bible to do so.

Disciples from the Inside Out

Embracing the way of the cross as the way of Jesus is to embrace the gospel of Jesus Christ. One of the challenges we face is understanding that the gospel is more than just our individual salvation, more than just getting a ticket to heaven. The gospel, which Jesus himself preached, has everything to do with Jesus and centers around his proclamation of the inbreaking kingdom of God (Matt 4:17; Mark 1:14; Luke 4:43) as well as the death, burial, resurrection, and ascension of Jesus. Christians rightfully are drawn to the death, burial, and resurrection of Jesus when thinking about the gospel, just as the apostle Paul does in the fifteenth chapter of First Corinthians.

As important as the events of Jesus' death, burial, and resurrection are to the gospel, they are the means through which the gospel becomes the good news. But to speak of these events as the entirety of the gospel or to speak of the gospel simply in terms of receiving forgiveness of sins is reductive. When Paul speaks about the death, burial, and resurrection of Jesus, he mentions twice how these events happened "in accordance with the scriptures" (1 Cor 15:3–4). There is a narrative that Paul is referring to when he mentions the scriptures, and it is this narrative within its entirety that tells us the full understanding of the gospel. To speak of the gospel, then, is to talk about the story of Israel, which God brings to fulfillment in Jesus Christ through His death, burial, and resurrection.[4]

Since the gospel we speak of is rooted in the story of Israel, the promise of salvation we have received is inseparable from the proclamation of the inbreaking kingdom of God. Our salvation, then, is more than just the forgiveness of sins and the promise of eternal life in Christ. Salvation is the good news of the kingdom, that God is reclaiming his rightful reign in and through the crucified and resurrected Jesus whom God the Father has exalted as the Lord and Messiah. This is the good news that declares the promise of salvation, including the forgiveness of sins and eternal life but also reconciliation to God and others as a new creation.

4. McKnight, *The King Jesus Gospel*, 61.

God's Artwork

At this point, though, we must understand this embracing of the gospel in relation to our calling as disciples, people who are following Jesus. In other words, embracing the gospel of Jesus Christ, with its promise of salvation, is to follow Jesus as a community of disciples otherwise known as *church*. Our commitment to living as disciples should characterize us as local churches so that we are learning to live by the same beliefs, values, and habits of Jesus, which is itself an ongoing activity. This life of following Jesus forms as our inner life so that our local churches increasingly become expressions of the inner life of Christ.[5] As the inner life is formed, which happens as the inner life of each individual disciple is formed in the way of Jesus, the outward expression will increasingly reflect the beliefs, values, and habits of Jesus. These expressions become an embodiment of the gospel in the local church.

For the formation of the inner life, we need to reflect some more on discipleship as a practice in the sense of a discipline. At the root of the word, *discipline* is the word *disciple*, which is about learning and receiving teaching so that discipleship becomes the way of life, the practice of each follower of Jesus and the church as a whole. This understanding of practice is a human activity that makes use of what Alasdair MacIntyre regards as internal goods, what could be regarded as a set of skills aimed at achieving an outcome based on those skills.[6] If we understand discipleship as a practice, then we undertake the practice of discipleship by embracing the particular set of beliefs, values, and habits that are internal to the practice. In other words, discipleship must proceed from these beliefs, values, and habits rather than any number of end goals or what MacIntyre speaks of as external goods.

Perhaps a more helpful way of understanding this concept of practice is knowing the difference between the games of baseball and softball. With both games, the end goal is to score runs and win the game. That goal requires baserunners, so in both baseball and softball, the batter is trying to

---

5. Willard, *Renovation of the Heart: Putting on the Character of Christ*, 22.

6. MacIntyre, *After Virtue*, 187, describes this definition of practice as "any coherent and complex form of socially established cooperative human activity through which goods internal to that form of activity are realized in the course of trying to achieve those standards of excellence which are appropriate to, and partially definitive of, that form of activity, with the result that human powers to achieve excellence, and human conceptions of the ends and goods involved, are systematically extended." See also Stone, *Evangelism after Christendom*, 31, who offers an analysis of evangelism as a practice involving various skills and techniques with internal and external goods.

get on base and score. Unlike the game of baseball where the baserunner may steal a base under the rules of the game, there is not any stealing of bases allowed in softball. If the baserunner in the game of softball is simply playing with the end goal in mind, a utilitarian approach in which the end justifies the means, the baserunner may decide to steal a base or two in order to increase his or her chances of scoring a run. However, doing so means that the baserunner is no longer adhering to the rules and isn't therefore really playing the game of softball anymore. To push the illustration a bit more toward the absurd, imagine if the batter in either softball or baseball decided to remain on base even after popping out to the third-baseman. Not only would this seem absurd, but the game itself would suffer credibility by a player trying to redefine the rules to achieve an end goal.[7]

This is the credibility loss the gospel suffers when the embodied life of the church is determined based on desired outcomes, such as church growth, rather than the practice of discipleship. Yes, the set of beliefs, values, and habits that form discipleship are more enigmatic and will always involve making certain interpretive decisions about the biblical text. Nevertheless, these beliefs, values, and habits are nonetheless essential.

When the Future Breaks into the Present

Though some disagreement remains among Christians as to what the necessary beliefs, values, and habits are that we must embrace as disciples, not all is beyond understanding. At the start, Christian discipleship is rooted in the mission of God and God's self-revelation in the person of Jesus. Hence, our understanding of church, with its embodied way of life (discipleship) must form our participation in the mission of God, which is fulfilled in Jesus Christ.

One of my favorite books on my shelf is Vincent J. Donovan's *Christianity Rediscovered*, which is now a classic missionary text for those engaging in cross-cultural evangelism. In the book, Donovan tells of his own journey in relearning the essentiality of the Christian Faith, and he came to the conclusion on this journey that the church participates in this mission

---

7. MacIntyre, *After Virtue*, 190. The point is that any practice involves both external goods and internal goods that define the sort of activities involved in a particular practice. These activities, and particularly the internal goods, are what MacIntyre calls "standards of excellence and obedience to rules" that the practitioner(s) must submissively accept in order to participate in the particular practice.

of God "insofar as it participates in the act of Christ, which is mission."[8] As Christians, we cannot separate mission from Jesus Christ who fulfills the mission of God, defining for us what it means to live on mission with God and how that life of mission is lived.

As followers of Jesus gathered into local churches, we are faced with a question of what it means for us to share in the life of Christ as participants in the mission of God. We receive some necessary assistance in answering this question from one of our basic affirmations of faith as Christians, namely our profession that there is one God who eternally exists in three persons: the Father, Son, and Spirit. The baptism of Jesus is one of those occasions where we unequivocally encounter all three persons of the Trinity at work. As Jesus comes out of the baptismal water, the Jordan River, the Spirit of God descends upon him and the voice of heaven, The Father, says "This is my Son, the Beloved, with whom I am well pleased" (Matt 3:17). Here we encounter the Father, Son, and Spirit working as One. This unity we encounter means that the ministry Jesus will undertake as the Son is done so in the power of the Spirit according to the pleasure or will of the Father. This is why Jesus will later tell his disciples that the Spirit will come to guide them into the truth, proclaiming what is from Jesus the Son and his Heavenly Father (John 16:12–16).

In the power of the Holy Spirit, Jesus undertook the will of his Heavenly Father, proclaiming the arrival of the kingdom of God. The obedience of Jesus led him to Jerusalem where he suffered a shameful and horrific death on the cross, and then after being buried in a tomb, he was raised from death unto life and then eventually ascended back into heaven. The life Jesus lived, proclaiming the kingdom of God and culminating in crucifixion, resurrection, and exaltation, makes a sweeping historical claim because the future is now known to us. Though every detail of the future is not known to us, it is known to us in the promise of hope. God, the Father, Son, and Spirit, has conquered sin and death, which then extends to us this victory by the means of Jesus Christ, our Lord (1 Cor 15:56–57). So, as followers of Jesus gathered together as local churches, our understanding of mission is not only anchored in Jesus but is shaped by the victory he has achieved, which is the basis of our hope.

This is to say that our understanding of mission and what it means to live on mission with God as followers of Jesus means becoming a *Christ-centered* and *Kingdom-oriented* mission. The fancier way of expressing this

---

8. Donavan, *Christianity Rediscovered*, 77.

Part Two: Discipleship and the Church

mission and our life of discipleship is to say that we are called to embody a life that is shaped simultaneously by both a *Christological* and *Eschatological* dimension. Christology is the aspect of Christian theology concerned with our understanding of who Jesus is and the life he lives, whereas eschatology, while technically referring to the understanding of the last things such as death and eternity, is our understanding of how the future of history is coming into existence. So, while our Christology is shaped by what God has accomplished in the crucifixion, resurrection, and ascension of Jesus Christ, this accomplishment is also what establishes the eschatological future of God's kingdom-reign that is breaking into our present history.

What we need to understand is that though the crucifixion of Jesus appears as the hideous end of Jesus, his resurrection and ascension redefine the cross as the proleptic victory of God. That is to say that the gospel events which transpired in Jerusalem are now viewed as a prolepsis in which this future victory is present to us as a fixed reality. We know the future, and so it seems that our embodiment of the gospel must reflect this future as a living reality.[9] Knowing this future, available to us by faith as the promise of hope, must also refashion the way we read the Bible, which is something we will explore more at greater length later. However, before we can do so, it seems necessary that we understand how our faith and hope must transform the way we live as followers of Jesus if we are to embody the gospel as Jesus has called us to do. This transformation is a way of life characterized by what Scot McKnight calls "Christoformity," which is a lived theology of "being conformed to Christ."[10]

As the church, we are to embody the gospel, which means that our lives are also conformed to Christ, his beliefs, values, and habits. By way of an example, taking this more seriously in our local churches might help us avoid some further leadership maladies that only seem to undermine the very gospel we profess as our faith and hope. What I have in mind here

---

9. Moltmann, *The Church in the Power of the Spirit*, 75, demonstrates how the church exists in relationship to Christ "as a factor of present liberation, between remembrance of his history and hope of his kingdom." For a fuller treatment of Moltmann's eschatology, see his first book *Theology of Hope*. Of particular interest here is Moltmann's description of hope as the reality through which Christians participate in the life and resurrection of Christ. "Thus resurrection is present to them in hope and as promise. This is an eschatological presentness of the future, not a cultic presence of the eternal" (p. 161).

10. McKnight, *Reading Romans Backwards*, 27, who also uses this expression in his book *Pastor Paul*, 4, where he also describes the expression by saying "we are called to be conformed to Christ. . . . we are formed by his life, by his death, and by his resurrection and ascension. We are not only to believe the gospel but also to embody it."

is the small but significant number of prominent evangelical pastors that have either resigned or were dismissed in the wake of various scandals. I don't have any interest in identifying any particular names, although a quick Google search will identify most rather easily. Nevertheless, I am not interested in that because it's not pertinent to the point I want to make, and there isn't any need to make any particular person the object of any voyeuristic pursuit.

What I am interested in is the fact that most of these pastors were serving in so-called megachurches, even multisite or multicampus churches. This observation is important but not because of the size or the way these churches "do church" per se. As an outside observer who also serves as a pastor, the issue, it seems, has more to do with a church model rooted in a practice that begins with an end-goal in mind, the external goods rather than the internal goods of discipleship defined by a set of beliefs, values, and habits. This is not to say that the pastors and the churches they served were bereft of living any sense of the Christian life; it's just that certain beliefs, values, and habits were set aside in order to achieve an end. Why so? Perhaps there are many reasons, but at least some of it has to do with the focus on numbers and how those numbers become the measurement for success, which means organizing the church around efficiency.[11] Every pastor knows the issue all too well because it's too often the basis for evaluating whether the church is successful and even if the pastor is good.

As a result, the end goal or the external goods of the church become church growth. Just from some of the books on my shelf, we can see how this objective has become the starting point for church planting and church renewal.[12] At face value, this doesn't seem to be a problem. What could be so wrong with seeking to grow a church? After all, ideally, a growing church means that more people are coming to faith in Christ. Well, assuming the best, that would most likely be true. However, because this objective begins with the end in mind in order to develop a plan for growing the church, the means is shifted toward an attractional church model. That is, build a church building or find a location to meet that doesn't look like a traditional church building, create a worship experience with a lot of lights,

---

11. Fitch, *The Great Giveaway*, 32.

12. Here is just a small sampling of such books, from particular books that are on my bookshelf. See Warren, *The Purpose Driven Church*; Hunter III, *How to Reach Secular People*; *Church For the Unchurched*; Mittelberg, *Building a Contagious Church*; Donahue and Robinson, *Building a Church of Small Groups*; Stetzer and Putman, *Breaking the Missional Code*; Stetzer and Dodson, *Comeback Churches*.

videos, and a very energetic praise band to go along with a relevant message delivered by a pastor who doesn't look like a traditional pastor but has a lot of charisma and clout to draw in the people.

Now, so that nobody misunderstands, this isn't to suggest that missional and attractional are inherently opposed. There isn't anything inherently wrong with gathering as a church in an unconventional-looking place or with using technology and having a praise band. The preaching certainly should speak to where people are at. However, when the utilitarianism of efficiency and attractiveness determines the means of being the church, the church is marketed as a brand. The pastor—with his exuberant charisma and clothing attire from Johnson & Murphy, Urban Outfitters, etc.—becomes the face of the brand, and the church grows on the strength of this brand. The pastor, along with a leadership team, increasingly focuses on strengthening and preserving this brand with the pastor functioning more like a CEO. So, instead of pastoral leadership formed and functioning from the lived theology of Christoformity, the leadership script is taken from the pages of American business.

Sound familiar? Of course, it does, and it didn't seem so problematic until it was, until certain pastors became domineering, manipulative, and abusive. Even more troubling is the way church leaderships ignored the signs of trouble percolating and even suppressed the complaints. And why, we might ask? Perhaps part of the reason has to do with allowing the end to justify the means of efficiency which meant protecting the brand until containment stopped working, until what was bubbling and bubbling began boiling over for everyone else to see.

How might things be different if the first duty of the church, including every pastor and other leaders, was following Jesus? What might it look like if the way that churches function proceeds from learning to live like Jesus, embodying his beliefs, values, and habits? What if our goal wasn't to grow a church but to simply live as disciples of Jesus, trusting God to bring about the results—the fruit of our labor in Christ?

A Portrait of Heaven on Earth

Flipping the script and living as churches whose calling is to follow Jesus does not mean that we will never be without sin again. However, embodying the gospel as followers of Jesus participating in the mission of God does mean cultivating the way of Christ. Such a life opens space for us to live

God's Artwork

and be present among society not as mere adversaries or allies but as witnesses.[13] We bear witness to the new creation we believe God is bringing from the future into the present existence, the new creation we already are in Christ (2 Cor 5:17). This presence will certainly require a new way of reading the Bible, but before we can explore what that might involve, we need to fully grasp what this life means for our identity in Christ as local churches among society.

As we come to Jesus in repentance and believing the good news of his kingdom, we live as followers of Jesus. Christoformity becomes our way of life so that the way we live is centered in Christ and oriented to the coming of God's kingdom. Yes, this life, with the inherited promise of salvation, comes to us as an invitation and something we receive only by grace. But as important as every spiritual blessing we have in Christ is to our life as the church, God has saved us so that we can also participate with him in his redemptive mission to the rest of the world. This is why Paul, after explaining how God made us alive again in Christ while we were dead in our sins, says that "God did this to show future generations the greatness of his grace by the goodness that God has shown us in Christ Jesus" (Eph 2:6).

This missional election in Christ means that we are saved by grace through faith for the purpose of good works, which Paul clarifies in Ephesians 2:8–10:

> For by grace you have been saved through faith, and this is not your own doing; it is the gift of God—not the result of works, so that no one may boast. For we are what he has made us, created in Christ Jesus for good works, which God prepared beforehand to be our way of life.

This is how God is at work in Christ. The language of election used earlier in Ephesians 1:4 is nothing new to the biblical narrative. Beginning with Abraham and continuing with Israel, the significance of election was always universal in scope, as God is choosing people to participate with him in his missional desire to bless all nations.[14] So, here in Ephesians, we are

---

13. Fitch, *Faithful Presence*, 27, says "God's presence is not always obvious. He requires witnesses. God comes humbly in Christ. He so loves us, he never imposes himself on us. Instead he comes *to* us, to be *with* us and in that presence he reveals himself. . . . *Presence* is how God works. But he requires a people tending to his presence to make his presence visible for all to see."

14. Newbigin, *The Open Secret*, 68; see also Wright, *The Mission of God*, 369.

told that God has saved us by his grace through faith[15] and though this salvation is not of our own doing, it will result in us doing good works if we truly grasp this grace of God. In fact, the result is that our life as the church following Jesus makes it evident that we are "God's accomplishment" rather than our own.

This chapter began with a discussion about art, and here is where our love for all forms of artistry connects with our calling to live as disciples, local churches embodying the gospel in our local communities. The word used by Paul to describe us as "God's accomplishment" is *poiēma*, which is where our English words "poem" and "poetry" derive from. English translations vary in the way they render this term, from "God's handiwork" (NIV), "God's masterpiece" (NLT), or simply saying that we are "what he has made us" (NRSV). What should be clear, though, is that Paul is describing us, as the church, by saying that we are God's poetry[16] which is just a way of saying that we are God's "work of art," (NJB) as the *New Jerusalem Bible* renders this passage.

Just think about what it means to be the artwork of God for a moment. As we follow Jesus, embodying the gospel in a manner that is centered in Christ and oriented toward the kingdom, God is painting a picture for the world of what the future will be when Christ comes again. Of course, the painting isn't complete, but as we engage in doing the good works that God has prepared for us, we become a living portrait of what the gospel—the good news of Jesus and the kingdom of God—really looks like. And yes, sometimes we can really smudge up the painting that God has done, leaving God to fix the messes we make. Nevertheless, when we receive the gospel and allow God to transform us from dead sinners into a living portrait of the gospel in Christ, we reveal the beauty of God's greatness.

I remember one night sitting over at my church's campus ministry house, Blue Hens for Christ, and one of our campus missionaries and I were talking with several students about how we see God at work. As we were

---

15. Traditionally, understood through the lens of the sixteenth century Protestant Reformation, the contrast between faith and works has been understood in a generic sense that is against any human merit. So as Schreiner, *Paul*, 210, describes faith as linked with grace since salvation is "based not on doing but on believing and trusting . . ." While such an understanding of faith is generally true, it seems to miss the context pertaining to the reconciliation of Jews and Gentiles. Dunn, *The Theology of Paul the Apostle*, 355 understands that the context of Jewish and Gentile reconciliation implies that Paul is contrasting faith with is the Torah, "the law required *of Israel as God's people*."

16. Hiebert, "God's Creative Masterpiece," 117.

talking, it occurred to me that neither of these students was following Jesus two years prior. Yet on this day, here they sat as followers of Jesus. One of them was sharing a story about helping another student who is struggling with faith, while another one was telling us how he is sharing his faith with a few other students that he works out with during the week. Finally, there was a nursing student sharing how she befriended some homeless people living in a shelter where she was doing a clinical, and here she sat telling us of how she started participating with them in a group Bible study. Such examples may seem small and may not automatically seem obvious, but together they all serve as another stroke from God's paintbrush, portraying his greatness and what the future will be when Christ returns.

Other times, the world encounters examples that point to something beyond the dismal conditions people face daily. For example, centuries ago, Christians caught the attention of the world through the charity they embodied and extended to others. The *Apology of Aristides*, written by a philosopher named Aristides who became a Christian, wrote about the church in the second century, saying:

> And when they see a stranger, they take him in to their homes and rejoice over him as a very brother; for they do not call them brethren after the flesh, but brethren after the spirit and in God. And whenever one of their poor passes from the world, each one of them according to his ability gives heed to him and carefully sees to his burial. And if they hear that one of their number is imprisoned or afflicted on account of the name of their Messiah, all of them anxiously minister to his necessity and if it is possible to redeem him they set him free. And if there is among them any that is poor and needy, and if they have no spare food, they fast two or three days in order to supply to the needy their lack of food.[17]

But even today, there are notable examples of how Christians embody the gospel in a manner that reflects the good news of Jesus and the kingdom of God.

About sixteen years ago, on October 9, 2006, a man by the name of Charles Carl Roberts entered the West Nickel Mines School, an Amish school in Lancaster, Pennsylvania. What followed was a mass shooting, resulting in ten girls being shot and five of them dying before Charles Roberts turned the gun on himself. Such scenarios, which happen all too often in America, evoke outrage. While the anger is understandable, most people

---

17. Aristides, *Apology*, 15.

Part Two: Discipleship and the Church

would never stop to consider how they will love their neighbor and much less the family of the gunman that just killed their children. Yet the Amish, who have a history of cultivating peace that is willing to love even their enemy as part of their embodiment of the gospel, did the almost unfathomable.

Instead of having to flee town in shame, as the parents of Charles Roberts thought they would need to do, an Amish Christian by the name of Henri showed up. He was there to tell the parents that they were not the enemy but were also parents grieving the loss of a child. From there, the Amish embraced the Roberts family as part of the community. And today, there is a room in the house of the Roberts home that was built as a gift by the Amish with the word "Forgiven" written above the double-pane window.[18]

Conclusion

When we encounter good artwork, whether in the form of a song, a painting, or something else, the art captivates our attention. We pay attention to that artwork, being filled with a sense of wonder as we draw inspiration and are even challenged to think and act differently. This is why we, as the church of Jesus Christ, exist. Our salvation in Christ means we gain the privilege of serving as a living portrait of the gospel, embodying that gospel in a manner that reflects the way of Christ and the coming of the kingdom that God has inaugurated in Christ. When we begin reading the Bible as a window for seeing Jesus and learning to live like Jesus, we learn how to live as God's artwork, reflecting his kingdom-reign upon the earth as it is in heaven just as Jesus did when He walked upon the earth.

As we encounter people who are caught up in the death traps of this world, be it their own sins or the injustices and evils they have suffered in a world enslaved to sin, what we have to offer is the promise of hope we have already received in Christ. That's an offer that only makes sense in words to the degree in which we coherently embody as our way of life. For this, Jesus is still calling us to come and follow him.

---

18. Itkowitz, "Her son shot their daughters 10 years ago. Then, these Amish families embraced her as a friend."

5

The Living Bible

A Library with One Story to Tell

> "The devil can cite Scripture for his purpose. An evil soul producing holy witness is like a villain with a smiling cheek, A goodly apple rotten at the heart. O, what a goodly outside falsehood hath!"
>
> —WILLIAM SHAKESPEARE

AFTER JESUS WAS BAPTIZED, the Spirit led Jesus into a wilderness where he was tested by the devil. We read about this testing in both the Gospels of Matthew and Luke, though the Gospel of Mark does also mention this period of testing after Jesus was baptized. While these tests are important for understanding the ministry Jesus undertakes as Israel's Messiah, I bring it up here only to point out the fact that in the story, the devil does recite Scripture to Jesus.

In the second test, the devil wants Jesus to jump from the highest place overlooking the temple in Jerusalem to see if God will save him from what would surely be his death. In an effort to persuade Jesus, the devil cites Psalm 91:11–12 to Jesus, saying, "for it is written, 'He will command his angels concerning you,' and 'On their hands they will bear you up, so that you will not dash your foot against a stone'" (Matt 4:6; cf. Luke 4:10–11).

Just think about that for a moment . . . The devil citing Scripture! The archenemy of God, the satanic power that is opposed to everything that is good and godly in creation, knows the Bible well enough to cite Scripture to Jesus. Perhaps we could get the devil to teach a Bible class at next Sunday's church gathering, maybe even preach the sermon too.

Of course, you and I both know that's the most preposterous idea ever. The devil may cite Scripture all he wants, but we see through his motives. Thankfully, so did Jesus. What the devil is actually doing is proof-texting and cherry-picking Scripture in the worst way, manipulating Scripture to his own ends in service to an agenda that is opposed in every way to the good news of Jesus Christ and the kingdom of God. But if the devil can do this, who are we to think that others, perhaps even ourselves, cannot misuse Scripture?

I once had a Bible professor say in a class that all a pastor needs to do is put a smile on his face and a finger on a verse. Really? Is it really that simple? I know what my professor intended. He certainly wasn't implying that we should go about manipulating people as a charlatan with a Bible and a smile to hide a devilish grin, but there are Christians who think knowing right from wrong is as simple as putting a smile on your face and a finger on a verse. If we think that is how the Bible works, then the next time your hand causes you to sin, go cut it off like Jesus said (Matt 5:30).

Okay, I'm being sarcastic, but you get the point. And yet there's hardly a week that goes by without hearing Scripture cited for purposes that have little to do with following Jesus as participants in the mission of God. All kinds of people do it, including pastors and theologians but also politicians and journalists, cultural critics and literary critics, and even the guy from down the block as he begins sobering up from last night's bender. Even the Klan, defending the antebellum south, would cite Scripture, which ought to make us pause again for some sober reflection. Yet, even with every political election and every controversial issue that comes down the pike, we will hear people cite Scripture in order to garner support from Christians.

One of my favorites is the way some people will try their best to make Jesus into a violent person in order to justify Christians engaging in violence. Some will mention how Jesus drove the animals out of the temple with a whip (Matt 21:12–14; Mark 11:15–19; Luke 19:45–48; John 2:13–16). Yet nowhere in the story do the gospel writers ever mention Jesus using the whip on people or acting with violence upon people in any other manner. Others, however, cite Luke 22 to mention how Jesus told his disciples to buy a sword (v. 36) as though that passage somehow justifies a Christian ethic of violence. What they fail to mention is how the very next verse tells us that Jesus told them to buy a sword as a fulfillment of the prophecy that he would be regarded as lawless (v. 37). They also fail to account for the lack of faith Jesus sees in his disciples and how later in the same chapter when Jesus was arrested and one of his disciples used a sword, cutting off the ear of another man, Jesus rebuked his disciples, saying, "No more of this!" (v. 51). My point isn't to engage the ethical question of if or when is ever right for followers of Jesus to engage in violence but to show some of the absurdities that can result from simply citing Scripture.

When I was an undergraduate Bible and Ministry major, I was taking a class on the Gospel of John. As we came to the second chapter and the miracle of Jesus changing the water into wine, the professor spent three entire class periods trying to convince the students that Jesus did not change the water into fermented wine with alcohol. His effort was all aimed at trying to teach us future pastors and missionaries that it was immoral for Christians to consume even the slightest sip of any alcoholic beverage. Despite some of the shoddiest articles available on the internet (yes, anyone can publish anything on the internet too) about the making of wine in Jesus' day, a little knowledge about the process of fermentation and a close reading of the story of this wedding in Cana, it's clear that the water Jesus turned into wine was fermented wine. But that's not even the point of the story, which is the point I am making. In numerous ways, we can cite the Bible, cherry-picking either a verse or a story, and use the Bible in ways for which it was never meant.

Beyond the Concordance

On a shelf in my office, I still have *The NIV Exhaustive Concordance*, which was given to me by my parents many years ago as a gift. I don't really use the concordance anymore, as it was based on the original 1984 NIV translation which was replaced by the 2001 *Today's New International Version* and then the Updated 2011 NIV. Nevertheless, concordances have proven to be a useful resource for people studying the Bible, until they're not.

What I mean is that reading the Bible for participation in the mission of God requires more than just a concordance reading of Scripture. We can look up a word like *prayer* or *preach* and read every verse in the Bible where those words occur in an English translation. Doing so will surely teach us something about praying or preaching and ideally, our little concordance exercise will encourage our faithfulness in following Jesus too. But if we

Part Two: Discipleship and the Church

stop here, are we really reading Scripture for the purpose for which Scripture was given?

I don't want to be misunderstood. Knowing the content of what the Bible actually says does matter. We can't read the Bible well if we don't know what the Bible actually says. However, we must go beyond just knowing what the Bible says and what it says on any particular subject. The Bible is given to us as a collection of writings divided into two collections called the Old Testament and New Testament. Knowing whether a particular scripture on prayer is in the Old Testament or New Testament does make a difference. Of course, these writings come in different literary genres (history, poetry, wisdom, prophecy, gospels, epistles, and apocalypse), which makes a difference too. Going even further, each passage of Scripture has a historical and theological context that must be considered as much as it is possible when we read Scripture.

Even with all the diversity and complexity that is the Bible, there is still one story being told that begins with Genesis chapter one and continues to the end of Revelation. The importance of reading the Bible as a complete story matters immensely. Reading the Bible with a concordance approach, and even the selective proof-texting, risks splintering the Bible into an incoherent text which can be made to mean almost anything with a little Christianese speak.[1] This is when we end up with a Bible that becomes congruent with the many different kingdoms of this world. But when we learn to read the Bible as a narrative, we read a story that is calling for our participation. Instead of performing the stories of the many different kingdoms of this world, we enter the story and live as an embodiment of the gospel.

The Bible as a narrative then presents us with a deep repository and reservoir of God's will and working, his unfolding mission, within history. Yes, the story is told through multiple voices in different settings and genres, spanning different covenants, and reading the Bible is like entering into a library, but it has one story to tell. From the first chapter in Genesis all the way to the end of the last chapter in Revelation, the Bible tells one unfolding story.

---

1. Smith, *The Bible Made Impossible*, 17, sees the splintering of the Bible as a reason for the rise in "a pluralism of interpretations," that is so prevalent among contemporary Christianity. That being said, it should not be assumed that a narrative reading of the Bible will yield a homogenous understanding among Christians. What a narrative approach should do is reduce some of the more glaring absorptions of the Bible leading to syncretism of the Christian Faith with some other system of beliefs—religious, political, or otherwise.

The Living Bible

As we read the story, though, we can't ignore how the different writers of Scripture tell their part of the story in different settings with different genres of writing. As a result, there are places where the Bible evokes what seems paradoxical. For example, Jesus tells us that he came to bring division upon the earth (Matt 10:34; Luke 12:51), and yet one of his most famous prayers is for the unity of his disciples (John 17). Or while the Bible affirms our value as humans created in the image of God (Gen 1:26–27) and Ephesians affirms our value in Christ as God's workmanship (Eph 2:10), Jesus at one point instructs us to regard ourselves as worthless slaves (Luke 17:10). Ignoring the complexity doesn't mean it's not there; it just means we are ignoring an aspect of Scripture as we have received it in the Bible. "Out of sight, out of mind" is just a lazy response that neither takes Scripture seriously nor respects Scripture as the word of God. So, in reading Scripture, we must be willing to engage the complexity, but this does not mean the Bible is beyond any confident understanding or that academics are the only ones who can truly make sense of the scriptures. What it means is that we must move beyond flat, selective, and one-dimensional readings of Scripture.

Yet this has seemed too difficult for some. It's still common to encounter Christians and churches who read the Bible with a concordance approach. Doing so has its consequences, some of which have already been mentioned. Sometimes the problem is made even more difficult by a selective concordance approach. In my own denomination, there are two passages that have been cherry-picked out of their historical and theological context to not only prohibit women from preaching or serving as an elder but have often been used to preclude women from serving in nearly every aspect of Christian ministry.

The two passages I'm referring to are 1 Corinthians 14:34–35, "women should be silent in the churches. For they are not permitted to speak, but should be subordinate, as the law also says. If there is anything they desire to know, let them ask their husbands at home. For it is shameful for a woman to speak in church," and then 1 Timothy 2:11–12, "Let a woman learn in silence with full submission. I permit no woman to teach or to have authority over a man; she is to keep silent." Homing in on the words *silent* and *silence*, some have argued that women were prohibited from even offering a prayer or reading Scripture in the presence of men. Uncovering the many problems with such a conclusion and application is bigger than the point we are getting at here. What matters here is the lack of any attempt in understanding the biblical text within its context (exegesis) and the discernment of what role these instructions have in churches living in very different cultural settings (theological praxis).[2] Another problem is that these two particular passages of Scripture are very far from the only biblical texts that speak about how women have participated in God's redemptive mission throughout history. The point here is to illustrate why we must move beyond such a flat and sometimes, perhaps many times, selective reading of Scripture.

The Bible We Read

One of the key passages of Scripture about Scripture is found in a letter attributed to the apostle Paul that was originally written to Timothy, a minister serving in Ephesus. In 2 Timothy 3:14–17, Paul commends the scriptures to Timothy, saying:

> But as for you, continue in what you have learned and firmly believed, knowing from whom you learned it, and how from childhood you have known the sacred writings that are able to instruct you for salvation through faith in Christ Jesus. All of Scripture is inspired by God and is useful for teaching, for reproof, for correction, and for training in righteousness, so that everyone who belongs to God may be proficient, equipped for every good work.

This text, especially verses 16–17, is perhaps the most oft-cited passage of Scripture for affirming the inspiration and authority of the Bible. However, used as a proof-text as it often is, the depth of what Paul is saying to Timothy gets overlooked.

---

2. Smith, *The Bible Made Impossible*, 70, raises the questions of theological praxis on this very issue of women serving in ministry and these particular biblical texts when he says, "Take, for instance, the passage quoted above about women being silent in church. Is that a direct command to Christians now? Or was that a case of a particular command directed toward a specific situation that is not relevant for women and churches today? Or does it reflect a biblical teaching that is true at a level of general principle (and, if so, which principle?) but that must be applied variously depending on the specific historical and cultural situation? Different Bible readers believe each of these views, whether or not they are consistent in working them out. But let us suppose that one of the latter two views is correct. How might we know that? By what standard or principle could that be determined? And then what are the other implications of that standard if it is applied consistently? Nobody seems to know, or at least to agree. Yet these questions often matter a great deal." However these texts are understood, his questions demonstrate why we cannot be content with a simple reading of scripture that assumes a universal application of what the Bible says.

The Living Bible

While questions about the inspiration, truthfulness, and reliability of Scripture are important, it's not the point Paul is making. Paul regards all Scripture as inspired by God without any qualification or defense and assumes that Timothy shares his same conviction. The questions often asked today regarding the inspiration of Scripture are rather modern in scope and rooted in the Enlightenment. Without dismissing the importance those questions sometimes have, if that is all we talk about when it comes to Scripture, we miss other important aspects, perhaps even more important aspects, of the Bible to our peril.

In fact, I am writing about reading the Bible because I believe that all of Scripture is God's word to his people and that all of Scripture is truthful and reliable.[3] It is also my assumption that if you are reading a book about reading the Bible out of an interest in learning to better read the Bible, you too share such a high view of Scripture. This high view does not mean that God has verbally dictated every word of Scripture as though he was speaking directly into the ears of each biblical writer. Some Christians will disagree, but a close reading of Scripture makes this position hard to sustain. By faith, we can trust that God was providentially at work conveying his will to the divergent writers of Scripture.[4] Not only was God providentially at work in the writing of Scripture, but he also was providentially at work among the historical church in forming the canon of Scripture we call The Bible.[5] This is also why we should read all of Scripture and take into account all of Scripture. God has providentially given us and preserved for us the Bible as his word to guide us and form us as we follow Jesus.

---

3. Although the language used to affirm the truthfulness and reliability of scripture is not without problems, I do affirm that all thirty-nine books of the Old Testament and twenty-seven books of the New Testament are infallible (meaning "not liable to deceive"), see Stanley J. Grenz, *Theology for the Community of God*, Grand Rapids: Eerdmans, 1994, 398.

4. Grenz and Franke, *Beyond Foundationalism*, 73, describe the way that God communicated to the writers of scripture as an illocutionary performance involving the Spirit speaking as an act where the intended will of God is communicated rather than a locutionary act in which the very words of scripture are the spoken words of God. In other words, saying the Spirit speaks through the Bible is not an affirmation of any verbal dictation theory of biblical inspiration.

5. McDonald, *The Biblical Canon*, 405, names six different criteria the patristic church used for determining what writings should be included in the New Testament canon (apostolic, orthodox, antiquity, and usefulness of the scripture as well as their adaptability and inspiration) to go along with the Old Testament canon the church already accepted as scripture.

Part Two: Discipleship and the Church

As Christians, all Scripture includes both the Old and New Testaments. Yes, historically speaking, when Paul spoke of "all scripture," he was referring to the Old Testament. Yet there isn't any reason for us to limit Scripture only to the Old Testament. By faith, we certainly believe the New Testament is every bit as much scripture as the Old Testament. In fact, the word for scripture in v. 16 (*graphē*) is used elsewhere in the New Testament as a description for both the teaching of Jesus (1 Tim 5.18), the writing of Paul (2 Pet 3.15–16), which are also regarded by Paul as letters for churches to read (cf. 1 Thess 5:27), exchange (cf. Col 4.16), obey (cf. 1 Cor 14.37; 2 Thess 2.15), and regards them as words taught by the Spirit (cf. 1 Cor 2.13). So, let's affirm the New Testament as scripture, but in doing so, let's not forget that the Old Testament is equally scripture as well.

By faith then, what Paul affirms about the Old Testament, both its nature and function, we can affirm for both the Old Testament and New Testament. That is, the entire Bible—the thirty-nine books of the Old Testament and the twenty-seven books of the New Testament—are "useful for teaching, for reproof, for correction, and for training in righteousness, so that everyone who belongs to God may be proficient, equipped for every good work" (2 Tim 3:16–17). This is the function of Scripture and why we must read the Bible as a word from God that forms us for worship and discipleship. The question we must ask when reading different books of the Bible is how does each book teach, reprove, correct, and train us? As pointed out, because the Bible contains different writings from different periods of history and different contextual settings, the various writings will function differently in the way they instruct us. Eventually, we will delve into how such a reading of Scripture is possible. For now, though, we must be ready to read all of Scripture.

Before moving on, there are two concerns that are necessary to press at this point. The first concern regards the habit of regularly reading the Bible. As Paul wrote to Timothy about the importance of Scripture, he does so reminding Timothy of the "sacred writings" (v. 15) he has known since his childhood. Part of reading the Bible well is being immersed in the scriptures and the life they envision—God's word and will. This is where regular readings of the Bible matter, which will be discussed in more detail in another chapter. Right now, it is just worth stressing that by immersing ourselves daily in Scripture, God is able to cultivate a deep well within us flowing from the totality of his word as he forms us by the Spirit to live as followers of Jesus. But without reading the Bible regularly, this cultivation and formation are about as likely to happen as becoming physically fit will happen apart from regular exercise and healthy eating.

A few years ago, I was talking with a church leader about the church, the Bible, and Christianity in general. It was an informal conversation, but the more we talked, the more this leader expressed a very rigid understanding of Scripture and a strong certainty about all of his convictions. He's not the first Christian I have encountered who was so dogmatic and sure of himself. Like the others, he was very critical and judgmental toward anyone holding a different view, didn't see things his way, or believed what he considered to be false doctrine—even damnable doctrine. Yet as the conversation shifted to reading the Bible, this church leader made a stunning admission and admitted that he only reads the Bible about once a week as preparation for the Bible class he teaches at his church. This reading of the Bible consisted only of reading the passages of Scripture relevant to the class he was teaching, which was a lesson prepared by someone else. I'm not against using a class curriculum prepared by others to teach a Bible class, but in this case, it seems that the Bible had become a text to master for a class and nothing else.

Reading the Bible only for the sake of teaching others and seemingly entrenching ourselves deeper into a rigid set of beliefs misses Paul's entire point. We must not only read the Bible often; we must let the Bible read us as often as we read the Bible. Before Scripture is the word of God to others, we must receive Scripture as the word of God to us. And just like a quality conversation with a friend only happens when we give the quantity of space for that to happen, the qualitative function Scripture is to have is only likely to happen when we make quantitative space to read Scripture as the word of God to us.

Another concern regards reading all of Scripture. By that, I mean reading both the Old Testament and the New Testament as the entire word of God, rather than prioritizing one over the other. Few Christians would reject the Old Testament as God's word, but in my experience, too many times the Old Testament is treated as less significant or of less importance. Or the Old Testament is read simply to mine it as a supportive text to the New Testament. It doesn't help either that we can buy "Bibles" containing only the New Testament along with Psalms and Proverbs included. Nevertheless, it seems like sometimes the Old Testament becomes the forgotten Bible.

I'm not saying that we read the Old Testament the same way we read the New Testament. However, treating the Old Testament as less important or significant, we are functionally in danger of discarding roughly three-quarters of the Bible. The problem also bears upon our understanding of the Christian Faith. I once sat in a cafe talking with another church leader who believed that the God of the Old Testament was different than the God of the New Testament, with the former being an angry God ready to judge the world and the latter being a God full of grace and love for the world. First, such a view overlooks the multiple expressions of God's grace throughout the Old Testament and his judgment within the New Testament. As a result, the reader ends up with a dualistic faith similar to that of a second-century Christian named Marcion. His dualistic view of God and the Bible came to be known as *Marcionism*, which held that the vengeful Hebrew God was different from and less than the loving and forgiving God of the New Testament. But Marcion and his belief were rejected by the larger Christian church as heresy.

The point here is not to pass judgment but to stress the severity of what might happen when we fail to read the entire Bible as the word of God. We must dwell in this word, let it read us, and let it form us as people who worship the living God and follow his Son, Jesus Christ.

The Bible Everyone Reads

When we get down to the brass tax of reading the Bible, it's about the way we live as followers of Jesus. More knowledge of the Bible matters not if what we know doesn't change the way we live. This is what Paul is emphasizing to Timothy as he reminds him about the importance of the scripture as instruction "for salvation through faith in Jesus Christ" (2 Tim 3:15).

Yes, salvation. Not just an idea or school of thought but salvation, and as we have already seen, our reception of salvation in Christ is into a new life that involves doing good works. So, in being baptized into Christ (Rom 6:3; Gal 3:27), to borrow from elsewhere in Paul's writings, we are raised into a new way of living—a life of being and doing. The Bible, then, is given to us, as Paul stresses its function, "so that everyone who belongs to God may be proficient, equipped for every good work" (2 Tim 3:17). We read the Bible not just for information but for our transformation. Our Bible studies, which my own church tradition loves to have, cannot be content merely to ask what the Bible says. When we read Scripture, we must always be asking of the text how our life must change if we are to take seriously what the text says. Even though the answer to such a question involves some hermeneutical

The Living Bible

decisions, the point is that reading the Bible should change the way we live, and that change should be visible in the good works we do.

The life of good works we live is where our salvation converges with the mission of God. Or think of the grace we receive in Christ, which also means the reception of the Spirit, whose power enables us to participate in the mission of God. This convergence of salvation and mission is the visible embodiment of the gospel, which then reveals the glory of God to the communities we live among.

The kind of life that the Bible reimagines us to live as we read it makes us what Michael Gorman describes as "a *living exegesis* of the gospel."[6] Exegesis refers to the interpretation or explanation of a particular text—in this case, the Bible, or more particularly, the gospel as revealed within Scripture. It is based on the preposition *ex* which means "out" as opposed to the word *eis* which means "into." So, when we read the Bible, we draw out (exegesis) what the scriptures say rather than read into (eisegesis) our own understanding based on biases and already held conclusions. As we exegete the scriptures in our reading and then begin embodying the text, we become this living exegesis or interpretation of the gospel. Or course, there is more involved in such a reading so that we might strive to offer a true interpretation, but the point here is that we read the Bible so that the life we now live in Christ becomes a life of doing good works. It's that simple and that challenging.

The simplicity is that we can begin living this life of good works done in Christ right now. We don't have to understand everything about the Bible to live according to what we know now. And while more knowledge—even incites learned from scholars and theologians—can always be helpful, we need not wait until we think we've perfectly understood the text (which never happens anyway). Just as the wisdom of God is revealed in what is weak and despised (1 Cor 1:27–28), we can trust God to work in spite of our mistakes. This doesn't mean we settle for mediocrity in our embodiment of the gospel, and we certainly should not tolerate living contradictions of the gospel, but we begin where we are with the confidence that God is at work among us. This is why—which I cannot stress enough—we all need to pick up our Bibles and read. The Bible was given to every one of us. But do so knowing that the Bible we read is not the Bible everyone is reading.

---

6. Gorman, *Becoming the Gospel*, 43. Referring to a previous work of his, Gorman describes the church as a "living commentary" of the gospel it performs, see *Cruciformity: Paul's Narrative Spirituality of the Cross*, Grand Rapids: Eerdmans, 2001, 367.

Part Two: Discipleship and the Church

So, what about the Bible that everyone else is reading? Some time ago, I preached a message on the text of 2 Timothy 3:14–17. The title was *The Bible That Everyone Reads,* and that title was chosen thoughtfully. Preaching is more than just standing before a crowd and speaking. It's a craft that involves deliberate thought and creative writing so that it might become a spoken word that encourages and challenges as necessary. In the development stage of sermon crafting, preachers are looking for a way (what we call homiletic structure) and an angle to drive home a point. Ideally, the point arrives in a move that catches the hearers by surprise, enabling them to reimagine the life that God is now calling them to live as they have heard the biblical text read and proclaimed. And yes, this is the work of the Spirit just as much as it is the Spirit working in the preparation and development of the sermon.

On this particular Sunday, I wasn't expecting the message to have any more impact than any other Sunday. But oh me of little faith . . . I learned that day never to underestimate what the Spirit can do when the word of God is proclaimed.

Here I was preaching on 2 Timothy 3:14–17, explaining why we must always be reading the Bible as a spiritual discipline. I explained how all Scripture was given as God's word to us so that we may live a life of good works. But here was the point I was leading up to: We read the Bible so that we may do good works because the Bible that everyone else reads is us. Now, what story will they read? What will they learn about God as they read us?

I didn't realize the significance of what I was preaching until Jennifer, who was part of the church I was serving with, walked up to me in tears. She was a Christian, but somewhere along the way, her attention was diverted from the way of Christ, resulting in some significant moral failures that included a few D.U.I. convictions. Now she was an alcoholic in recovery trying to learn how to follow Jesus again. As she approached me, it became clear that a proverbial light switch was now on. With tears in her eyes and excitement in her voice that I had not heard before, she said, "I get it. We read the Bible so that others will see the gospel of Jesus Christ living in us."

Yes!

We read the Bible so that the gospel of Jesus Christ will be seen in us. We read the Bible so that we may embody the gospel by living a life of good works. We read the Bible so that the good works we do will begin to tell the good news of Jesus Christ and the kingdom of God. We read the Bible so that, to paraphrase Jesus, others will see our light shining and begin giving glory to God (Matt 5:16).

Conclusion

Mark Twain once said, "If Christ were here there is one thing he would not be—a Christian." I'm not sure what one of the great American writers saw that would provoke such a statement. Yet sadly, we know there are plenty of examples within history where such words proclaim the truth. But we can't go back and undo what has been done—not in our own lives nor in the lives of others throughout history. And becoming cynical isn't a good option either. What we can do is to take what we have been given, our salvation in Christ, and live out that salvation as followers of Jesus participating in the mission of God.

This is where the entire Bible matters because participating in the mission of God assumes that we are coming to know the story that reveals God's unfolding mission. Not only does reading the Bible matter, but recognizing that both the Old and New Testaments are a part of the story is important too. Nobody thinks they will fully understand a story if they skip parts of that story. Besides, the Bible itself teaches us that we need all Scripture rather than just some. And just as I was writing this, I was reading a comment on Facebook in which a Christian was complaining about the legalistic tendencies of his church and attributed the problem to spending too much time reading the Old Testament. Perhaps so, but I doubt that's the problem. I digress.

When we read the entire Bible as a story, the Bible begins to read us. If we're open, we become a living exegesis of the gospel being told throughout the biblical narrative. This is our embodiment of the gospel, a life that is observed by others through our good works so that they may begin to see the glory of the living God. That's why we read the Bible, but to truly embody the gospel in a meaningful sense to the people around us, there are still more questions to answer about the way we read the Bible. That is what awaits us in the next section.

Part Three

A Missional Reading of Scripture

6

Back to the Bible

A Narrative Reading of Scripture

"Thy word is a lamp unto my feet, and a light unto my path."
—PSALM 119:105 (KJV)

THAT IT WAS A warm and sunny spring day in Denver, Colorado, is not a surprise at all. I just remember this one particular day sitting outside a Starbucks reading my Bible because of the man who approached me. Since it's a good bet that if you're reading a leather-bound book, then you are likely reading a Bible, this man asked if that is what I was doing.

"Sir, is that there a Bible you're reading?" he asked, to the best of my recollection.

"Yes, it is. Why do you ask?" I responded as I was adjusting a chair for him to sit so that we could talk.

"Well, you know that it says in the Bible that President Obama is the devil. All of them. President Bush, President Clinton, President . . . and President Nixon."

Trying to be polite as this man sat down at the table with me, I said, "Hmmm . . . I must have missed the scriptures where their names are mentioned."

He didn't even detect the sarcasm in my response but proceeded to tell me what the Bible says about these former American Presidents. You

Part Three: A Missional Reading of Scripture

might be thinking this person is not playing with a full deck of cards, that he's a few bricks shy of a full load. Maybe he was. I certainly thought so at first. But the more I talked with the man, who was very polite throughout the conversation, learning that he was divorced but had children, worked as a local carpentry-contractor, and belonged to some sort of Pentecostal church, I realized that he was as normal as anyone else, including myself.

What wasn't normal was the way he read the Bible. Or maybe it wasn't so abnormal after all because he wasn't the first person, nor was he the last, to cherry-pick scriptures from the Bible to make them fit his own religious narrative, which just happened to be framed by a very dystopian view of American society and her elected Presidents.

The conversation is a reminder of what happens when we extrapolate Scripture from its own narrative and why we must recover a narrative reading of the Bible.[1] However, doing so is not simply a matter of opening the Bible and reading. The Bible is a little more complex than that, simply because its writings include multiple authors, different genres of writing, multiple occasions that span different historical periods of time, and all within a cultural worldview that is very different from ours today. I am not saying or suggesting that the Bible can only be read and understood by scholarly experts in the fields of biblical studies. However, just as we need someone to serve as a guide when we travel to a different country or visit someplace unfamiliar to us, so we do need some guidance in reading the Bible. The challenge is that some people, like the gentleman I met outside of Starbucks, are familiar enough with the Bible that they neither see the need for further guidance nor see how they could be misunderstanding the Bible.

Perhaps the best place to begin with trying to recover a narrative reading of Scripture is with an admission that we can misread Scripture and need help so that we might more faithfully read the Bible within its narrative. Such an admission is called *epistemological humility*, which simply means that we acknowledge our limitations in what we know and whatever knowledge we have obtained, and the conclusions drawn could require some change based on new information. My hope is that the previous chapters have at least made it clear that there is a need for change so that we might learn to read the Bible as a narrative. If a narrative reading of Scripture is

---

1. Recovering a narrative reading of scripture began gaining traction, at least in academics, with the publication of Frei, *The Eclipse of Biblical Narrative*. See also Placher, "Hans Frei and the Meaning of Biblical Narrative," 556–59.

not possible, then we'll continue allowing "the Bible to become fragmented [and] it is in danger of being absorbed into whatever *other* story is shaping our culture, and it will thus cease to shapes our lives as it should."[2]

One Story: Genesis to Revelation

Some time ago, I had the opportunity to meet with a college student that was a part of the church I serve with and was very involved in our campus mission. She was a senior expecting to graduate and in the throws of exploring options for graduate school, which meant in all likelihood, she would be relocating. So, she wanted to talk about different churches and how someone goes about deciding what kind of church to participate with when moving to a new city. A good question, indeed.

As we talked, she asked, "How do you read the Bible? I mean, how do you read it so that you're not just cherry-picking Scripture to make it say whatever you want it to say?" My eyes lit up even more. As many times as I have encountered misuse of the Bible, I relish another Christian asking me about how to read the Bible.

We briefly began talking about the importance of knowing the who, what, when, and where of the Bible, which is all to say that context matters. So, let me emphasize that: Context matters! The Bible is like a library collection of writings that are all contributing to one story, but knowing where a particular book is located in the Bible and the circumstances or occasion the book is addressing makes a difference. Notwithstanding the historical questions about authorships and dates, knowing who the writer is addressing and the general idea of what circumstances the audience is facing makes a difference. The canonical location of the writing within the Bible and the kind of writing genre make a difference.

To most, this all makes sense when explained. But as the student I was speaking with was nodding in agreement, I told her that we also need to read the Bible as one big story or narrative that begins with creation. Like any story, the biblical narrative has a setting and plot that involves different characters as well as a conflict that leads to a resolution. From start to finish, we encounter a story with many twists and turns but pressing forward toward one goal, with many smaller stories becoming one coherent book we call the Bible.

---

2. Bartholomew and Goheen, *The Drama of Scripture*, 12.

Part Three: A Missional Reading of Scripture

Although the exact structure of these acts is open for discussion, the basic breakdown involves five acts: Creation, Fall, Israel, Jesus, and Church/Consummation.[3] At the same time, the Bible is also a kingdom story that moves in what Scot McKnight describes as an A-B-A' story. This story begins with (A) God ruling as king over his creation through his covenant with Israel but with Israel wanting her own earthly king, (B) the reign of God is ignored until (A) the coming of Jesus who inaugurates the restoration of God's reign.[4]

In The Beginning: Creation—Genesis 1–2

The story begins with *creation* in the first verse of the Bible: "In the beginning God created the heavens and earth" (Gen 1:1). The creation account sets the stage for us as the readers, giving us the context for the conflict and resolution that will come later in the story. But one problem many readers encounter is getting lost in conversations about the scientific development of creation, which is not what the creation narrative is addressing. As important as such questions may be to us today, Genesis was written in a pre-scientific era, and other than telling us that God is the one who has created life, the story doesn't provide the scientific answers to how creation has come into its present existence. The narrative is interested in giving an account of who created us, who we are as created human beings, and what it means to be human creation. The answers to these questions do not depend on the acceptance of a literal twenty-four-hour and seven-day young earth creation.[5]

The creation narrative affirms that God alone has created. He is the Creator who is so powerful that he brings life into its habitable existence by his spoken word. The act of creation differs from other accounts of creation within the Ancient Near-Eastern world. Whereas the other accounts of creation assumed a polytheistic view in which the gods brought

---

3. This is an adaptation of the five-act model proposed by Wright, *Scripture and the Authority of God*, 122. See also McKnight, *The Blue Parakeet*, 73–74, who labels the five "elements" as Creating, Cracked, Covenant Community, Christ, and Consummation; Bartholomew and Goheen, *The Drama of Scripture*, 27 who divide the story into six acts consisting of Creation, Fall, Israel, Jesus, Church and Completed Redemption.

4. McKnight, *The Kingdom Conspiracy*, 28–35.

5. A good place to begin understanding the background of the creation narrative, based on the textual evidence understood within the Ancient Near-Eastern context, read Walton, *The Lost World of Genesis One*; *The Lost World of Adam and Eve*.

about creation through wars, making violence a part of the natural created order, Genesis is monotheistic. There is only one God, and this God is so powerful that he simply speaks creation into existence; violence doesn't have any part in this created order of life. And the life that this God has created, he considers as good.[6]

While creation is the beginning of life, we will eventually see that it's not the goal of life. For now, though, the creation account of Genesis first proclaims that we, as human beings, are created in the image of God. Both male and female, we all equally bear the image and likeness of God (Gen 1:26–27). No other animal or object in creation bears the image of God— just us. Second, as icons of our Creator, we are people of immense worth because we bear the divine image.[7] It's why God pronounces the sixth day of creation as "very good" (Gen 1:31). It is also why we are created with vocational responsibility toward the rest of creation. By multiplying and ruling over creation, we serve with God, benevolently caring for his creation.[8] In doing so, we participate with God, as servants of our King who care for his kingdom so that life might flourish for all of creation.

Lastly, we learn that God has created us to belong in a community relationship. When God says, "Let us make . . ." we hear the activity of the Father, Son, and Spirit. The image of God we bear is that of One God who eternally exists in a triune community of three persons. We are made for relationships, living as a community with God and each other. This is why God also created Eve, a woman as a "helper" for man.[9] Creation is com-

---

6. Osborn, *Death Before the Fall*, 29, The affirmation of creation as good is not a claim about the moral quality that life begins with or that creation is perfect, as the word *tob* (good) and *tob me'od* (very good) is describing the "qualities of beauty, worthiness or fitness for a purpose but never absolute more or ontological perfection." Osborn also notes that there were other words in the Hebrew vocabulary available to describe the English sense of "absolute perfection" if that was the intention.

7. The human reflection of God is rooted in the divine image (*tselem*) which is a term of royalty that implies that humanity bears an immense self worth, see Sarna, *Genesis*, 12. Sarna illustrates the self-worth of man by pointing out that the willful killing of any other creature is not considered murder but the willful killing of a human being is considered murder.

8. Grenz, *Created for Community*, 75, rightfully mentions that rather than humans using this vocational task as an opportunity for exploiting creation for their own selfish ends, people are to "mirror for the sake of creation the nature of the creator."

9. The Hebrew word *ēzer* rendered as "helper" is also used elsewhere in the Old Testament to describe the Lord as Israel's helper (Duet 33:39; Hos 13:9). Using this passage as a proof-text to claim that women are created to be in subordination to men or are somehow inferior to men is a profound misuse of the text as nobody would suggest that

pleted with the formation of a human community that multiplies and cares for creation so that life may continue to flourish.

Descent into Slow Death: Genesis 3–11

The book of Genesis continues with Adam and Eve, introducing us to the conflict in the story. We read how both man and woman were given the freedom to eat the fruit of every tree except for the "tree of the knowledge of good and evil" (Gen 2:17), for doing so will result in death. As the story goes, a serpent comes along and convinces Adam and Eve to eat of this forbidden tree. The ploy is that they will become like God and know the difference between good and evil, and so they eat.

We call this the fall, but it's really a descent into a slow death. By death, I'm not speaking in biological terms. The sin of Adam and Eve is a sin we all share in, and it's a sin that reorients our life with theological and sociological consequences. Instead of remaining subject to the rule of God, in whom life continually flows from like a spring of water, it is an attempt to live by our own rule. We become the arbitrators of what is right, but we fail again and again.

Starting with Adam and Eve, they're found hiding in fear from God, the very benevolent Creator who has given them life. But now they are banished from the garden God has placed them among. Creation in Genesis is depicted as a cosmic temple and sacred space in which God dwelled among his creation, including humanity.[10] Sin has changed what God created, with life becoming an existence of enmity and strife.

The descent into death continues with the very next scene in which Cain kills his brother Able. We've gone from the creation of a benevolent community flourishing with life to an existence in which brother will kill brother, an existence that keeps repeating itself over and over again. Violence and evil erupt and become such a part of this story that God actually repents, becoming "sorry that he made humankind on the earth, and it grieved him to his heart" (Gen 6:6). As a result, God sent a destructive flood upon the earth to destroy what he had created and sort of begin anew by saving a man named Noah and his family, along with various animals. This scene, the story of Noah's ark and the great flood, not only reveals how

---

the word helper implies elsewhere that the Lord is subordinate or inferior to Israel.

10. Walton, *The Lost World of Genesis One*, 82; *The Lost World of Adam and Eve*, 116–17.

angered God is by the evil that people do but also reveals the grace of God in his choosing to preserve human life. Although even with this reset, our story is one of vain persistence in elevating ourselves as a god.

The conflict of the story is filled with such hubris that people want to make a name for themselves by building their own habitation, a city with a tower that will reach the heavens (Gen 11:4). Such plans are just another way in which humans have rebelled from their created intent, resulting in the Lord scattering humanity and confusing their language.

At this point, we can see how the conflict between God and humans seems futile. After all, we will never be God, and God will never allow us to subvert his sovereign place no matter how much we try. But the conflict also raises a question: Since humanity was created to participate with God as his servants in bringing about a flourishing life but has failed thus far, how will this problem be resolved?[11]

A Redemptive Vision: Genesis 12–Malachi

God is God, and we are not. So, should God have chosen to do away with human existence at this point, writing us all off as a lost cause, that would have really been his prerogative, but he didn't. In fact, our rebellion against God has never caused him to stop loving us. We begin to discover how gracious and merciful God really is when he calls upon a man named Abram, also called Abraham.

As God calls upon Abraham, he sends him to another land with the promise that he will make a great nation of him. As Abraham is full of faith, God enters into a covenant with Abraham, promising him that all nations would be blessed (Gen 12:2–3; 17:3–5; 22:16–18).

In keeping his covenant promise to Abraham, God eventually calls upon a man named Moses to lead Israelites out from the oppressive slavery in Egypt. Why is God doing this? Because he has chosen to make the Israelites his people who will serve as "a priestly kingdom and a holy nation" (Exod 19:6). After doing so, God enters into a covenant with Israel, becoming their Lord and leading them into a land he had promised to Abraham.

---

11. Beale and Kim, *God Dwells Among Us*, 40, "Instead of Noah as a second Adam expanding the sanctuary of God's presence by filling the earth with images of God, the earth is filled with a people so rebellious that they are dispersed 'over the face of all the earth' (Gen 11:9). The unabated spread of sin after the flood raises a question: How will the commission of Adam ever be fulfilled in light of the prevalence and power of sin?"

Part Three: A Missional Reading of Scripture

It is through Israel that God will rule as King again, as he demonstrates his power to deliver Israel with a crushing victory over the mighty Egyptians. However, we also see the grace of God revealed as the deliverance of Israel was an act of mercy on the part of God. It is why Israel came to know God as "The Lord, the Lord, a God merciful and gracious, slow to anger, and abounding in steadfast love and faithfulness" (Exod 34:6; cf. Num 14:18; Neh 9:31–32; Pss 86:15; 103:8; Joel 2:13; Jon 4:2).

The establishment of Israel as a nation further reveals the mission of God and the redemptive vision he is pursuing. In keeping his covenant with Abraham to bless all nations, God has blessed the Israelites to be their own nation so that they will be the vehicle through which God blesses all nations. That's what it means to be a priestly kingdom and holy nation. It's an important detail in this section of the story if we're to understand our own place in the story. We'll never understand the story as it unfolds in the New Testament as it was intended unless we have a good understanding of how the story is told in the Old Testament. So, it's important to see that Israel was called to serve the Lord as a kingdom of priests and therefore serve as a light to the nations (Isa 42:6; 49:6). Election, then, which is what God has done in choosing Israel to fulfill his promise to Abraham as a missional act, calling Israel to live as participants in the mission of God.[12]

As the people of God, Israel is called to live in obedience to God, worshiping no other idols and keeping the Law (Torah) that he gave them. Yet the human propensity to reject God is still a part of this story. Over time, Israel sought to be like the other nations and have their own king, rejecting God as their king (1 Sam 8:4–9). Even in appointing a human king to rule over Israel, they failed in keeping the covenant with God. Israel became a dynasty under the reign of King David, and because God promised David that a descendant of his would always be upon the throne of Israel, his son Solomon followed David as Israel's king. It was King Solomon who built the first temple in Jerusalem, but following Solomon, Israel and her kings became rebellious.

This eventual result was a division of Israel into two kingdoms, both of which came under the judgment of God and were taken captive by the Babylonians and thus were exiled among the nations. The Temple that King Solomon had built was destroyed, and now the Israelites were forced to live

---

12. Wright, *The Mission of God*, 369, "We cannot speak biblically of the doctrine of election without insisting that it was never an end in itself but a means to the greater end of the ingathering of the nations. Election must be seen as missiological, not merely soteriological."

under pagan authority. Even though their exile eventually came to an end and they were able to rebuild the Temple, they remained living under the rule of pagan authorities. However, for all the words of judgment spoken by Israel's prophets, the prophets also proclaimed a message of hope that one day the Lord would restore his kingdom.

Jesus Christ and the Kingdom of God: Matthew–Acts 1

By the first century, a prophet named John the Baptist came along, proclaiming the coming of God's kingdom, calling the people throughout Judea to a baptism of repentance for the forgiveness of sins. John was preparing the way for the coming of the Lord. And of all people, Jesus himself came to be baptized by John in order to fulfill righteousness. As Jesus was coming out of the water, the Spirit of God descended upon Jesus as a voice from heaven spoke, "This is my Son, whom I love; with him I am well pleased" (Matt 3:17, NIV).

Following his baptism, Jesus endured a period of testing in a wilderness just as Israel was tested in the wilderness, but unlike Israel, Jesus remained faithful. Coming out of this period of testing, he began his public ministry in Galilee by proclaiming the good news or gospel, announcing, "The time is fulfilled, and the kingdom of God has come near; repent, and believe in the good news" (Mark 1:15). Jesus also begins calling people to come and follow him, learning from him how to live under the inbreaking reign of God.

We gain a glimpse of what this restored kingdom will look like when Jesus enters a synagogue in his hometown of Nazareth. According to the Gospel of Luke, Jesus takes a scroll of the prophet Isaiah and reads the portion that says in 4:18–19:

> "The Spirit of the Lord is upon me,
> because he has anointed me
> to bring good news to the poor.
> He has sent me to proclaim release to the captives
> and recovery of sight to the blind,
> to let the oppressed go free,
> to proclaim the year of the Lord's favor."

Hearing such good news should draw jubilant applause, especially as Jesus then declares that this scripture has come to fulfillment. But as Jesus went on talking about how God sent neither the prophet Elijah to Israel during a

Part Three: A Missional Reading of Scripture

famine nor the prophet Elisha to any of the lepers in Israel but instead to a Gentile named Naaman, his fellows Jews became angry—so angry that they wanted to kill Jesus.

What is really important here is what Jesus is saying about the kingdom of God. The restoration of God's kingdom wasn't just for Israel, as this promise also included the Gentiles. Knowing the story of the Old Testament and how God chose Israel to be the people through whom he would fulfill his promise to Abraham, we shouldn't be surprised here. Now this Jewish man named Jesus, an Israelite, is fulfilling Israel's calling. The kingdom of God Jesus is inaugurating is fulfilling the redemptive mission of God for all people—every race, tongue, and tribe. The promise of the gospel is the blessing of salvation unto all nations.

Salvation can mean many different things, like eternal life, the forgiveness of sins, new creation, reconciliation, and much more. Such ideas are found throughout the New Testament, but to understand better what such salvation promises mean, we must see the kind of life Jesus lived. To say it another way, to understand the kingdom of God that Jesus proclaims as good news, we must visualize the manner in which Jesus embodies the kingdom. That means paying attention to the way Jesus lives and listening to what he teaches.

We encounter the heart of his teaching, the characteristic vision for what the kingdom of God is to be, when Jesus delivers what we know as the "Sermon on the Mount" in Matthew chapters 5–7 (cf. Luke 6:17–49). As Jesus proclaims this message, he's casting a vision for how his followers are to live in the kingdom of God, bringing about a flourishing life.[13] Ironically enough, Jesus begins the sermon by pronouncing a series of blessings. Although the word *makarios*, with each pronouncement to follow, is used to describe what kind of people are happy, it's not a stretch to say this is the life that God blesses us to live.[14] While I understand asking God to bless us, the nation, etc., the pastor in me also wants to remind us that God has already blessed a life for us to live, if we'll follow Jesus.

As we do follow Jesus, the vision of the kingdom becomes even more clear as Jesus goes about teaching and performing numerous miracles. This is how the first disciples began believing that Jesus was indeed the Messiah

---

13. Pennington, *The Sermon on the Mount and Human Flourishing*, 36.

14. These pronouncements are naming the "privileges" of being citizens of the kingdom of God, see John R.W. Stott, *The Message of the Sermon on the Mount*, The Bible Speaks Today, Downers Grove: InterVarsity Press, 1978, 33–34.

(which means *Christ* in Greek) that the prophets spoke of. However, participating in this kingdom with Jesus is more than just a matter of believing he is the one sent from God to usher in the kingdom. Jesus also begins teaching about the suffering unto death he would endure, being crucified on a Roman cross, and that God would raise him from death.

The first disciples didn't understand, and we shouldn't assume we understand any more than they did. That's because the cross up ahead wasn't merely an event that had to happen but the way of life Jesus embraced and the way, as he insists, anyone following him must embrace. Following Jesus means we must be ready to deny ourselves, take up our own cross, and then continue following him, with the paradoxical assurance that our lives will be saved by losing our lives for Jesus.

It's easy to read about Jesus speaking of his own death and resurrection in the Bible and still misunderstand how this climactic event must characterize our lives as we follow Jesus. In the Gospel of Mark, Jesus speaks of his impending crucifixion three times, and a pattern emerges with his disciples misunderstanding the significance followed by Jesus correcting them (see Table 1). What Jesus insists upon is that his disciples must be willing to give up their own lives, including whatever privileges or rights, to go on living as humble servants to others. The caveat is that such discipleship is where life in the kingdom of God is found (Matt 16:24–45; Mark 8:34–35; Luke 9:23–24), which is realized as we follow Jesus into Jerusalem for the Passover.

Table 1: What Discipleship Means			
Gospel of Mark	**Chapter 8**	**Chapter 9**	**Chapter 10**
Prediction of Death	v. 31	v. 31	v. 33–34
Disciples Fail to Understand	v. 32–33 Peter Scolds Jesus	v. 33–34 Who's the Greatest?	v. 35–39a Sit by Jesus in Glory
Jesus Corrects the Disciples	v. 34–38 Self-Denial	v. 35–37 Be the Least of All	v. 39b–45 Be One Who Serves

By now, we are beginning to understand what it looks like to live out the two great commands of loving God and loving our neighbors as ourselves (Matt 22:36–40; Mark 9:28–31; Luke 10:25–28). We also understand the importance of living as servants who love each other (John 13:1–17, 34–35; 15:12), as this is the way in which the rest of the world will know that we follow Jesus. But now, in Jerusalem, where Jesus continues to challenge the authority of Israel's religious leaders, the religious authorities became resolute in getting rid of Jesus.

All four gospels tell us about the arrest, trial, crucifixion, and resurrection of Jesus. After his arrest, Jesus was brought before the Jewish Sanhedrin where he was condemned for death and brought before the Roman Governor Pilate, who questioned Jesus and then handed him over to be whipped and crucified. The crucifixion itself was a barbaric spectacle of humiliation intended to send a message about what happens to those who oppose Roman authority. How Jesus was bringing about the kingdom of God by being crucified didn't make sense until God raised Jesus from death and exalted him as the Lord and Messiah.

The crucifixion, resurrection, and exaltation of Jesus become the pivotal point of the biblical narrative. For us who believe, everything has changed. The world and the historical trajectory life seems to be following for so many is revolutionized. A new era has begun right in the midst of the old, spawning hope for the future ahead.

The Church and the Kingdom of God: Acts 2–Revelation

Still, the question of when God is going to restore his kingdom remains. That's the question the Israelites were asking after their exile in Babylon and the question they were asking when Jesus began proclaiming the good news of the kingdom of God. Even after his resurrection, his first disciples were still concerned about when God would restore the kingdom. Jesus told them not to worry but instead wait to receive the power of the Holy Spirit because he was sending them on to live as his witnesses (Acts 1:6–8). That's when Jesus ascended into heaven, leaving the disciples retreated to spend time in prayer and prepare for the mission ahead.

Fifty days after the Passover came the Day of Pentecost, but this was unlike any other Pentecost celebration. On this day, according to Acts 2, God poured out his Spirit, and the apostle Peter spoke up to proclaim what was happening and why it was happening. What was happening was that God was pouring out his Spirit on all people, both men and women, just as the prophet Joel had once prophesied about. Why was this happening? Because of Jesus, the same Jesus whose credentials were revealed through powerful miracles, wonders, and signs that God performed through Jesus during his life. This Jesus is the one that the Jewish leaders, conspiring with the Roman authorities, had crucified but whom God then raised from death and exalted as the Lord and Messiah. And now God is calling everyone to repentance and baptism in the name of Jesus Christ with the promise of receiving the forgiveness of sins and the gift of the Holy Spirit.

We now begin to see the significance of the life, crucifixion, resurrection, and ascension of Jesus as well as the outpouring of the Holy Spirit. A new creation in which all people—Jew and Gentile, Slave and Free, Male and Female—identified by their baptism have become equals in Christ, signified by baptism (Gal 3:28). The promise which God made long ago to Abraham has now become reality, all because of the redemptive grace and mercy of God. This is why the letter to the Ephesians says, "You are saved by God's grace because of your faith" (Eph 2:8, CEB). This grace of God manifested in Christ reconciles all people to God and each other as one new body of Christ called the church.

As the church, our life is one of good works, characterized by the life Jesus lived himself and possible by the power of the Spirit. Rather than living by the stories and values of the old life, we are a new creation in Christ participating in the story that God is fulfilling within history. We live our confession that Jesus is Lord, that all authority is given to Jesus, expressed in holiness and humility. So, as difficult as it may sometimes be, we renounce sinful behaviors and replace those old ways with the new way of Christ by loving and serving one another as well as extending forgiveness to each other just as the Lord has forgiven us. We teach this story and how to participate in the story to everyone who comes to faith in Jesus Christ, so that they too will live as his followers and serve as God has gifted them to do so from his Spirit.

This is how we participate in the mission of God. And as exciting as it is, it's far from easy. Our life as the church—our beliefs, values, and practices—sets us apart from the rest of society. In fact, sometimes our non-believing neighbors may oppose us directly or indirectly. We shouldn't be surprised, since that happened to Jesus too, but it is a reminder that as followers of Jesus, we are "aliens and exiles" (1 Pet 2:11) among the world. That's true whether we live in America, China, or anywhere else in the world.

This is why we continue meeting as brothers and sisters, worshiping and fellowshipping together. Doing so provides opportunities for singing and praying together, hearing the word of God, and receiving instruction and encouragement as the word of God is proclaimed. Most importantly, though, we gather to share in what we call the Eucharist or Lord's Supper in which we share bread and wine to remember the death and resurrection of Jesus. In doing so, we not only offer praise and thanksgiving to God, but we are being reminded of the story we are not a part of.

We know this story, what has happened, and where it's going. We know that we share now in the future of God's redemptive goal. Knowing this goal and the story it belongs to allows us to live proleptically, portraying what's to come in the here and now as living witnesses of Jesus.

A New Heaven and a New Earth

Now, about that future to come . . . Throughout the New Testament, we are given enough bits and pieces to know that it will be a bodily life. Just as Jesus, as the "first fruits" (1 Cor 15:20) of the resurrection of the dead, experienced a bodily resurrection, so we will be raised as people with bodies too. The difference is that we will no longer have corruptible and mortal bodies that are subject to decay due to sin and death. Instead, we will be raised with glorious bodies that are incorruptible and immortal.

This is our victory in Christ which by faith is present to us now as our "living hope" (1 Pet 1:3). The promise of this hope will be revealed in its fullness on the day Christ returns to earth. All who have experienced physical death will be raised back to life, followed by those who are still living.

It's true that we don't know when this day will be. Even though it may seem far off in the future, there are certainly times when we will desire this coming day to happen "soon and very soon," as some of us used to sing in our youth groups. However, the biblical narrative ends similar to the way it began, with God dwelling among us in the holy city where the glory of God will be its light. There the tree of life will be, and this life, illuminated by God, will last forever. We are simply told that Christ, the one who testifies to such things, is coming soon. And compared against the eternity of forever, his coming will be soon. Our response is simply to say, "Amen. Come, Lord Jesus!" (Rev 22:20).

Epistles of Christ

One of those goals I set for myself at the beginning of 2020 was to read through Fyodor Dostoevsky's novel *The Brothers Karamazov*. In book 2, there is a chapter titled, "A Lady of Little Faith" that talks about an elder named Father Zosima urging a wealthy lady to practice love, striving to love her neighbor without ceasing. The lady responds by talking about her desire of caring for the poor. As she talks, Father Zosima admonishes any such romantic notions, saying, "love in action is a harsh and dreadful thing compared with love in dreams."[15]

In a similar vein, embodying the gospel can be a rather difficult and messy endeavor compared to any romantic notions in our dreams we have about following Jesus. Participating in the mission of God always sounds exciting when we talk about it, but in reality, it is a life filled with twists and turns, ups and downs, that can be more difficult than we ever imagined. As many pastors can attest to, there are times when turning and walking away at least momentarily comes to mind. It has nothing to do with the lack of faith—it's that living the faith we profess sometimes hurts. Yes, every follower of Jesus knows that the road ahead will not always be easy, but when the journey gets rough, resilience can seem like hell.

Doing the right thing and making the right decisions is never easy and sometimes very difficult. At the beginning of 2020, I am sure many people had plans already mapped out—conferences, family vacations, school objectives, and on and on. But you know what they say about the best-laid plans . . . most of which all got tossed out the window once the COVID-19 coronavirus became a pandemic. First came social distancing, then came sheltering in place and the shutdown of all non-essential businesses, and that included any gatherings of more than ten people, which meant church as we knew it was no more. At least, not for a while.

Like many organizations, churches faced the challenge of how to press forward when gathering for worship and life groups was not an option anymore. Challenges like that are why knowing the story we are a part of matters so much. We know from reading the story that the vehicle God chooses to further his mission is always people, and that's what the church is. At first, I briefly wondered how the church I serve might survive, but then I quickly remembered that the church I serve is neither a building nor a place and time; it's people—a community of believers following Jesus.

Yes, like many churches, Newark Church began gathering online for worship and fellowship. We formed connection groups meeting together through Zoom and Google Meet so that we could continue encouraging one another and learning to follow Jesus together. Opportunities for serving our community, such as making sack lunches for our neighbors in need of a meal and sharing some medical masks we received to local nursing

---

15. Dostoevsky, *The Brothers Karamazov*, 58.

homes and nearby apartment complexes, continued. Doing so wasn't even a question because we know how the biblical narrative goes, and so we know the story we are living.

In my own church tradition, the Churches of Christ, a man by the name of David Lipscomb lived as a preacher and educator in Nashville, Tennessee. During the summer of 1873, an outbreak of Cholera spread through the city of Nashville, causing many deaths and sickening many more. As we all know now, such outbreaks of disease also wreak havoc on the economy, and those who are among the poor suffer the worst.

Lipscomb was upset with the way many Christians were leaving the city rather than trying to care for the sick. The problem as he saw it was a failure among Christians to practice their religion when it mattered most. In his response, exhorting Christians to go beyond a mere profession of Christian Faith, Lipscomb wrote:

> Man is baptized out of himself, out of the world and its institutions, and is baptized into Christ that he may walk in him, obey him, enter into his spirit and that Christ may be formed in him. He thus becomes one with Christ, he is in him, he acts through him. The pledge that we solemnly make in our profession of faith in Christ and of our baptism into him is, that we will strive to reproduce his life before the world in our own lives. Hence we are epistles of Christ to the world, to be read of all men.[16]

This response is worth noticing because his reasoning proceeds, rather than precedes from, his Christian Faith. The point that Lipscomb makes is based on more than just a few *ad hoc* passages of Scripture. It's what happens when we are immersed in the narrative of Scripture, in which we understand that the Bible is not just providing us information and details about our Christian Faith but is actually serving as a script that we live among the world—hence, the importance of understanding the story Scripture tells and draws us into as participants who live as "epistles of Christ to the world."

Conclusion

How does anyone summarize the Bible in one chapter of a book? Well, I have given it a good college try. In doing so, I am aware that my efforts or anyone else's effort involve some editorial work as well as some exegetical

---

16. Lipscomb, "The Cholera and the Christian Religion," 649.

and theological decisions. That is, I cannot mention every detail mentioned in the Bible and still summarize the story it tells. Doing so also means making some interpretations about what Scripture says and what it means. So, there will always be room for further discussion about whether my, or anyone else's, retelling of the Bible narrative is accurate, but it would be a shame to get bogged down in such discussions and mistake a tree for the forest.

We can always go back and revise our retelling of the story as we gain a new understanding. What is important is that we are able to retell the story because it seems unlikely that we will ever live out of a story we cannot tell in our own words. So perhaps the first step in embracing a missional hermeneutic, in reading the Bible as a Christ-centered and Kingdom-oriented story so that we may embody the gospel as Christ-centered and Kingdom-oriented participants in the mission of God, is to start summarizing the Bible as a story ourselves. Get together with a few other Christians and share your retelling together, offer feedback, and revise as necessary. Then anticipate what good works God will accomplish through your entrance into the story of Scripture with a renewed gospel imagination for participating in the mission of God.

7

Renewing Our Imagination

Entering the Gospel Story as a Church

"The word of God can require something of me today that it did not require yesterday; this means that, if I am to hear this challenge, I must be fundamentally open and listening."

—HANS URS VON BALTHASAR

My generation, Gen X, grew up hearing the phrase "a mind is a terrible thing to waste." What is now a part of our American vernacular was a slogan first used by the United Negro College Fund in 1972. The idea behind the slogan was the promotion of equal education and opportunity for all people regardless of race. Eventually, the slogan seems to have become a way of encouraging all children in school to value learning and the education they're receiving.

Admittedly, I didn't always embrace the value of learning as I do now, but wonders never cease, as my fifth-grade teacher always said. That said, it's a terrible thing to waste our minds. Education matters, but more than just graduating with various degrees and obtaining more knowledge, we must learn how to think about what we know. That's true for the various vocations we undertake as a job, and it's true for our Christian Faith as well.

Learning how to think about the Christian Faith typically begins with reading the Bible. As stressed throughout this book, we must learn to read the Bible so that we may faithfully but contextually embody the gospel as participants in the mission of God. Reading the Bible, then, requires more than just knowing what the scriptures say. In the Gospel of Luke, after the resurrection, Jesus began speaking to his disciples about his life as the fulfillment of Scripture, and in doing so, "he opened their minds to understand the scriptures" (Luke 24:45, CEB).

As people committed to following Jesus, we need our minds opened to understand Scripture. We know the story told from Genesis chapter one to Revelation chapter twenty-two, and the gospel proclaimed within these pages of Scripture, but what shall we do with the story? The answer, to which we focus our attention now, has everything to do with how we think about this story. So, let's think some about the gospel as it's told within Scripture.

The Thinking Mind of Christ and His Church

Before we do, let me share another quick memory from my youthful years. I was generally a well-behaved boy growing up, but like any child, I wasn't perfect. There was that time when my younger brother and I, along with another friend, decided to build a fort by sawing the branches off of this weeping willow tree in the yard of a house that we thought was abandoned. We pretty much destroy that tree in our efforts at building the coolest fort ever.

As it turned out, the house wasn't abandoned. The owner just happened to be one of those retirees that traveled south from Indiana to Florida every winter. We obviously didn't know that and never even gave it any consideration.

Needless to say, when my parents found out, I swear that smoke began emanating from their heads as their disgust with what we did intensified. My brother and I wound up grounded for a long time, and the allowance money I was saving for a guitar was diverted to help pay for a new tree. At one point, though, I remember one of my parents indignantly asking, "What were the two of you thinking?"

Well, you might say that we weren't thinking. But that's not exactly true. We were thinking; we just weren't thinking in the right manner and without any wisdom whatsoever. My mother used to always tell us, "Just think about what you're about to do and ask yourselves, 'Would my mother like it if we do this?'" But that never occurred to us then, so we needed to be corrected. Not just punished, though we needed and deserved that too, but disciplined in the truest sense of the word—taught to make better

Part Three: A Missional Reading of Scripture

choices, wiser decisions. This was even true with the *WWJD* slogan asking *What Would Jesus Do?* that became popular in the late 1990s. We can make Jesus out to do just about anything, including killing[1] if we're not careful. Answers to such a question do require some discipline in the way we think about such matters and the sort of actions that such matters may demand.

In his book *How To Think*, Alan Jacobs suggests that the analytical power we employ in our thinking requires character. For Jacobs, the kind of character he has in mind is the capacity to turn our analyses into both "positive thought" and "meaningful action."[2] Although I do not disagree, character for Christians and churches must be Christ-formed. We need to develop a character that is formed after Christ by both the life he lived as well as his crucifixion, resurrection, and exaltation. Such life-formation was a concern for the Apostle Paul throughout his writings in the New Testament. More than just addressing the circumstances of different churches and reminding them about the gospel, Paul also sought their transformation into Christlikeness. The aim of such formation was that these churches might better appropriate the narrative of the gospel and therefore embody the gospel more faithfully. This embodiment of the gospel is the kind of positive and meaningful action required of Christians and churches.

Such character formation requires the transformation of the mind, altering the way we think in a manner that opens new space for imagining what it means to embody the gospel. This is why after spilling much ink to talk about God's work of salvation in Romans, Paul urges the church to offer themselves as a living sacrifice unto God. But how does such meaningful action happen? The answer is by not conforming themselves to the world but instead by being "transformed by the renewing of your minds, so that you may discern what is the will of God . . ." (Rom 12:2).

Elsewhere in the Pauline writings, similar points are made about our minds. The same word for mind (*nous*) used in Romans 12 is also used by Paul to describe those who are spiritual as having "the mind of Christ" (1 Cor 2:16) as well as putting away our old selves and having our minds "renewed in the Spirit" (Eph 4:23). Such renewal and transformation require

---

1. I recall a conversation about the ethics Christians engaging in violence and warfare, as it related to the threat of terrorism. During the conversation, one individual who was adamant that killing a terrorist was moral, said that it is what Jesus would do. When asked on what basis did he believe that Jesus would kill a terrorist, the person said that since Jesus is God Incarnate, Jesus was the one killing the enemies of Israel in the Old Testament.

2. Jacobs, *How to Think*, 43.

new thinking (*phroneō*) rather than thinking as the world (Matt 10:23; Mark 8:33). It requires us to think less of ourselves (Rom 12:3) and instead more as Christ (Rom 15:5; Phil 2:2). The character formation we need is the work of God, a gift of his grace to us, but it requires our receptivity in an intentional manner that becomes a "concentration of mind and heart."[3]

As the COVID-19 coronavirus pandemic began to spread across America, a lady from the church I serve was kind enough to be concerned about my health and well-being. So, she bought be a bottle of Vitamin C—the *Ester-C* brand, which I'm told is a high-quality brand. All I needed to do was take one of these vitamins each day. Since I'm not a pharmacologist, I didn't have any clue as to how effective doing so might be in preventing COVID-19, but I figured it would still benefit my health in some way. So, I took Vitamin C every day.

Now, in taking this Vitamin C, was I responsible for making myself healthier? In one sense, we might say yes; I had a choice to make and did in fact choose to take the Vitamin C. However, answering yes to the question is also short-sighted. Saying that I'm responsible for whatever health benefits were gained in taking the vitamin is a failure to see the providential blessing of God at work. I would never have taken the vitamins had I not received them as a gift from another person, and as a matter of faith, I also believe that God was benevolently working through this lady. Even when I was taking the vitamins, their effectiveness was not because of my own doing. So, taking the vitamins was not me earning or achieving for myself; it was receiving a blessing of better health from God through another individual.

The same is true with our receptive participation in our own character formation and the way that affects the life we live as followers of Jesus, including the promise of salvation. God has blessed us with Scripture as well as other people, in whom he is at work so that our life will be formed in the way of Christ. We can choose to resist that blessing or receive that blessing by intentionally participating in the activities that form our character after Christ. Choosing to do so, as we all should, is not earning or achieving anything for ourselves. Instead, we are receiving God's blessing as his continued offering of grace to us.

---

3. Charry, *By the Renewing of Your Minds*, 53.

Part Three: A Missional Reading of Scripture

Entering the Narrative of Scripture

The more we are transformed in the way of Christ, the more we begin to see the world around us through the lens of the gospel as revealed in the narrative of Scripture. Although God works through his Spirit within different people and experiences we encounter in life, it's hard to imagine such transformation without Scripture. This is why reading the Bible matters so much. Doing so shapes our understanding of the gospel and opens space for us to reimagine what embodying the gospel might require, both as individuals and as local churches.

When faced with questions about church and ministry, the first place we usually turn to for answers is the Bible. With a Christ-formed mindset and an awareness of the biblical story, we seek answers. Though our quest will most likely involve reading other books, listening to some podcasts, and even attending a conference, at the end of the day, what matters is what Scripture says. However, we must keep in mind that we cannot and shouldn't attempt to go back and do church as we see it done in the Bible. Likewise, reading Scripture shouldn't be about trying to recapture some other perceived golden era of the church. What we need in the twenty-first century are fresh expressions of local churches embodying the gospel in manners that are understandable within their own local contexts.[4]

Let me explain what I mean about (mis)reading the Bible to reproduce a presumed church order from the Biblical text. This happens when Christians, well-intentioned for sure, read the Bible in a manner that ignores both the contexts behind Scripture, the occasions for which the various writings were originally written. Assuming a monolithic church pattern in the New Testament, an appeal is made to Scripture on the basis that church renewal requires reproducing everything about the New Testament church pattern. In other words, the *function* of the church participating in the mission of God depends on the correct *form* of the church—the first-century pattern in particular. Whether talking about worship, church leadership, mission, evangelism, or something else, the idea is that everything will be fine if we just do everything exactly as it was done then.

At face value, this pattern approach seems plausible and even desirable when faced with a church that seems only to be circling the drain. However, the problems that exist in many struggling churches often

---

4. McKnight, *The Blue Parakeet*, 28, rightly says "What we most need is not a return to the first or fourth or sixteenth or eighteenth century... We need twenty-first century Christians living out the biblical gospel in twenty-first-century ways."

have little, if anything, to do with ecclesiological form. So, returning to a "simple church" or "house church" model because that is what we read in Acts 2:42–47, which is an idealized portrait,[5] solves little, if anything. The church, universally and locally, is people, and so it is always susceptible to problems regardless of its form. Certainly, there are places and occasions where decentralizing from a building and fellowshipping instead as a web of "missional communities" meeting in homes may open space for greater participation in the mission of God. However, such a conclusion should not and cannot be made simply because that appears to be the model we encounter at the beginning of the church. The same goes for worshiping together and our organizational leadership because we are living in completely different contexts.

That said, I'm not suggesting that we are free to live as we determine and that our churches are free to make everything up as we go about participating in the mission of God. We must read Scripture and take what it teaches with the utmost seriousness, but to embody the gospel in a manner relevant to our own cultural context, we must enter into the pages of Scripture as participants within the grand storyline told throughout the Bible. This is how we, as followers of Jesus, become a living embodiment of the gospel and thus a living Bible to others around us. Herein lies the importance of knowing the story the Bible tells, as we focused on in the previous chapter.

Instead of reading the Bible as a flat text with arbitrary commands and teachings, we read the Bible as a story. This approach, a narrative hermeneutic, began gaining traction with Hans Frei's publication of *The Eclipse of Biblical Narrative*. In reading the story, we encounter life as God sees and the way that God is remaking and restoring life in Christ. The vision we receive as we read the story cultivates within us a new medium, that is a culture and language, that forms our imaginations.[6] It is in encountering this new medium that we are transformed into the way of Christ and there apt at embodying the gospel we proclaim.

At this point, we need to understand that the formation, or (re)formation, of our imaginations happens only as we enter the story. The narrative generated by the biblical story has its own rationale and directives for the

---

5. Johnson, "The Acts of the Apostles," 61.

6. Lindbeck, *The Nature of Doctrine*, 33, describes the narrative as a "cultural and/or linguistic framework or medium that shapes the entirety of life and thought. . . . It comprises a vocabulary of discursive and nondiscursive symbols together with a distinctive logic or grammar in terms of which this vocabulary can be meaningfully deployed."

way in which the story must go. This is why we must enter the story of Scripture as opposed to applying Scripture to our lives, yet the latter is what happens many times when Christians read the Bible together. My retirement would likely be set if I had a dollar for every time I had someone ask me how what I'm preaching or teaching applies to their life. Subtly, though, in seeking application, we become the arbitrators of what works in Scripture for our lives. That makes us consumers of Scripture, which is at our disposal, rather than participants seeking to embody the gospel revealed in Scripture in submission to King Jesus.

By entering the narrative of Scripture, the question is not whether what we learn works with our lives but instead how we live the text as it is revealed within the story. As this happens, we encounter the Living God and his work that is past, present, and future. This opens the reality of life as God sees, which is centered in Christ and oriented toward God's kingdom. This encounter calls us and opens space for our lives to change direction, following instead the path for which all of history is moving toward and how that path is revealed in Jesus. By entering this story in submission to Jesus as Lord, we begin to understand our true selves, the life we have been created to live, and how we are to live that life as followers of Jesus and the gospel he reveals.[7] In this way, we are not seeking to apply or make Scripture work with our American lives but are instead living the life that is imagined within the narrative of Scripture in light of the gospel revealed as we reside in America (or whatever nation we reside among).

Honesty with the Truth

Admittedly, entering into the narrative of Scripture and living the life it imagines in Christ is easier said than done. Our formation as followers of Jesus is an ongoing journey, one of many twists and turns as well as steps forward and backward as we face the challenge of discipleship. Embracing this challenge requires us to become honest with the truth—the truth of ourselves and the truth revealed in Christ.

---

7. Fitch, *The Great Giveaway*, 143, contrasts preaching for application with narrative preaching, which is preaching that calls the hearers to entire into the narrative of scripture. With narrative preaching, he describes the preaching task as "to unfurl the reality of who God is past, present, and future so that all men and women who would submit to live in that world would then be able to understand themselves, who they are, where they are going, and what they are to do in terms of Jesus Christ and his story."

Renewing Our Imagination

The quest for truth, however, is a challenge itself. We live in an age of pluralism where there are numerous competing claims for truth, in religion and other aspects of life. The Oxford Dictionary's word of the year for 2016 was *post-truth*, which says a lot about the challenges that seeking truth presents. In the following year, during an interview on *Meet the Press*, Kellyanne Conway was attempting to defend White House Press Secretary Sean Spicer against accusations of making false claims by saying that Spicer was simply offering "alternative facts."[8]

Logically, truth is not capricious and varying. Yet it is in some sense because our truth is whatever we believe as true, and when confronted with anything different, we resist. Back in 1992, Rob Reiner directed a movie called *A Few Good Men*, a fictional story about two US Marines on trial for the murder of another Marine named Santiago. The murder was part of an unofficial order called "Code Red" that came from Colonel Jessup, who is commander of the base. Lieutenant Kaffee, the JAG lawyer representing the two defendants, is questioning the Colonel on the witness stand, asking him if he ordered the Code Red. Demanding an answer, he says, "I want the truth." That's when Colonel Jessup shouts out, "You can't handle the truth."

That is one clever way of diverting attention away from the truth—in this case, the truth that Colonel Jessup is responsible for the murder of Santiago. This diversion allows Colonel Jessup to stand by his own code of ethics in which this murder is justified for the greater good, even though it's obvious to everyone else that he's in the wrong. It's the same tactic Pilate used with Jesus when he asked, "What is truth?" (cf. John 18:38) Instead of Pilate seeing the Truth that's staring him in the face, he subtly changes the conversation so that he can carry on.

That's the challenge we face when it comes to truth. We live in a pluralistic society where many different stories are told. We tell these competing stories as they are, and our truth becomes the stories we tell ourselves—true or not. By story, I'm talking about the way we define ourselves, how our life begins, and the trajectory or plotline that our life takes us on toward the end we have in mind. We tell ourselves these stories enough that we begin to believe them and live them as the truth.

Somewhere along the way, we encounter Jesus and the gospel he reveals. This encounter challenges what we have accepted as truth so that we

---

8. Blake, "Kellyanne Conway says Donald Trump's team has 'alternative facts.' Which pretty much says it all."

Part Three: A Missional Reading of Scripture

may receive the Truth. We can see how this encounter works in the story of the apostle Paul.

Though we mostly know this Apostle as Paul, his Hebrew name is Saul, and he wasn't always the great missionary for Christ that we know him to be. Known as Saul of Tarsus, he was a devout Pharisaical Jew who persecuted followers of Jesus. In fact, that's what Paul was intending to do as he traveled to the city of Damascus, but it was on that journey that Saul/Paul encountered Jesus (cf. Acts 9, 22, 26). Or more accurately, Jesus confronted Paul.

Realizing that Jesus was indeed the Lord, Paul had what we call a conversion experience, but it wasn't just "getting saved." This conversion was a recognition of the truth that allowed Paul to be honest with the truth of himself. By his own words in Philippians 3:5–6, Paul had a Jewish pedigree that made him superior among his fellow Jews. He was circumcised on the eighth day and was of Israel and the tribe of Benjamin, making him a Hebrew among Hebrews. He was also a Pharisee, which meant he was devoted to keeping the Law (Torah). He was even able to boast about his devotion to his faith, attested by his persecution of the church and righteousness under the law that made him blameless according to the law. That's the truth, according to Paul, the Jewish story he told himself. This was the truth that Paul lived his life by, and he thought he was right until he encountered Christ.

The result of this encounter with Christ was what we might call a collision of truths for Paul. He had to contend with the truth of himself, namely that he was wrong. What he believed was right and what he thought made him righteous was in fact wrong. In being honest with the truth of himself, accepting that he was wrong, Paul was able to receive the Truth of Christ. We know this because Paul says, "These things were my assets, but I wrote them off as a loss for the sake of Christ" (Phil 3:7). In fact, the truth conversion that Paul has experienced is so profound that he comes to regard all of these assets, in comparison with knowing Christ, as "sewer trash" (CEB).[9]

Although the notion of sewer trash may disgust us, it also helps us understand the value Paul places on what he once regarded as truth in comparison to knowing Christ. That is because knowing Christ, for Paul, means participating in the light which Jesus has inaugurated through his

---

9. Silva, *Philippians*, 157. Most translations render the word *skubalon* in rather tame English, such as "rubbish" (NRSV) or "garbage" (NIV). However, the abrasive nature of this term may imply, as Wright suggests, that it is best translated as *crap* or *shit*; see Wright, *Justification*, 149.

crucifixion and resurrection.[10] As Paul will say in Philippians 3:10–11, "I want to know Christ and the power of his resurrection and the sharing of his sufferings by becoming like him in his death, if somehow I may attain the resurrection from the dead."

Regarding the lives we live now, we confess that there is only one truth, the Truth known to us as Jesus Christ. Though other stories masquerade as truth, we have been deceived by them, just as Paul was deceived. There are many deceptive stories we might tell about ourselves. They might be capsulated in simple statements such as "I'm worthless" or "I'm ugly." Other times, these deceptive stories run very deep and complex, whether they are the stories embedded in racism, sexism, and so forth. One of these stories that many people live for as though it is the truth is the American stories—not one story, but multiple stories competing with each other— that Americans tell. However, our encounter with Christ must be allowed to confront us with the truth that places the American story in its place in comparison to knowing Christ. I'm quite sure Paul would list the American story right along with the Jewish story he told himself, as something to be regarded as sewer trash.

Either Jesus Christ and the gospel he proclaims is true or it is false. If we confess the former, which is part of what identifies us as Christians, then the American stories we tell ourselves, whether written in red or blue ink or with any other ideological pen, are a loss. These stories are certainly not what we should be fighting for, as though participating in those stories is going to embody the gospel. As we come to this realization, space opens for us to receive what is indeed true. Encountering Christ makes it possible for us to see the truth.[11] With this new vision, the alternative stories we have believed become a loss so that we can embrace the Truth. When this happens, we are free to begin reading Scripture and entering into the life it imagines within the narrative as participants in the gospel of Jesus Christ. This is becoming honest with that truth, in which the Spirit leads us into repentance so that we may indeed become an embodiment of the gospel.[12]

---

10. Dunn, *The Theology of the Apostle Paul*, 487. See also N.T. Wright, *Paul and the Faithfulness of God*, 990, points out how "'Participation in the Messiah' and 'the forensic declaration 'in the right'' are both part of a single whole. And that single whole is covenant membership, and its redefinition through Messiah and spirit."

11. Hart, *The Beauty and the Infinite*, 333.

12. Gorman, *Becoming the Gospel*, 43, describes this as "a *living exegesis* of the gospel.".—-, *Cruciformity*, 367, where he rightfully says, "This people, the 'Church', lives the story, embodies the story, tells the story. It is the living exegesis of God's master story of

Part Three: A Missional Reading of Scripture

Conclusion

In Christ, God has called us and redeemed us to live in a relationship with him as participants in his mission. As it should be, our understanding of how we participate in the mission of God will always be formed by our understanding of Scripture. Reading the Bible, though, as we have already seen, always involves interpretation, which is shaped by the lens through which we read the Bible.

This book believes that in order to more faithfully participate in the mission of God as local churches within our local communities, we need to read the Bible as a grand narrative. That's because the story the Bible tells, centered in Christ and oriented toward the kingdom of God, is the true story that God is fulfilling within history. Telling the story within the pages of Scripture forms our minds so that the story becomes our story that we begin living as followers of Jesus. However, because we are living in the twenty-first century rather than any past period of Christianity and because our local churches exist within different communities with their own unique sub-cultures, our participation must also be shaped by the local context if it is to make any sense. That raises the question of how we actually read Scripture so that our participation in the mission of God is both faithful to Jesus and contextualized to our local settings. That is the question we must turn our attention to in the following chapter.

---

faith, love, power, and hope."

8

Living Gospel

A Faithful but Contextual Performance of the Story

"I never liked jazz music because jazz music doesn't resolve. But I was outside the Bagdad Theater in Portland one night when I saw a man playing the saxophone. I stood there for fifteen minutes, and he never opened his eyes.

"After that I liked jazz music.

"Sometimes you have to watch somebody love something before you can love it yourself. It is as if they are showing you the way."

—DONALD MILLER

SEVERAL YEARS AGO, I was interviewing different church leaders regarding research into how the Bible is read among churches. My assumption was that everyone hears the Bible read at some point during a worship gathering. Whether it's one of the readings for that week in the Lectionary or just an individual passage selected from Scripture, every church I am aware of has some reading from the Bible during worship. I also assumed that church leaders will read the Bible if they are teaching a Bible class or something similar. So, my interest was to know how often church leaders read their Bible just to read the word of God in Scripture, to encounter Christ and the kingdom of God, whether reading from the Old Testament or New Testament.

Part Three: A Missional Reading of Scripture

It's not that reading the Bible to prepare for teaching a Bible class is wrong. I mean, if I were leading a small group Bible study on Jesus' *Sermon on the Mount* in the Gospel of Matthew, then surely, we'll spend some time reading and rereading Matthew 5–7. Ideally, we're still hearing the voice of God speak. But when we read the Bible just to hear God speak, without any particular agenda or task other than to read Scripture, we might just be more open to the work of the Spirit forming us as followers of Jesus.

Now we're getting to an essential facet of reading the Bible for participation in the mission of God. I'm talking about our formation as followers of Jesus, which is very important if, when reading the Bible, we hope to discern how the Father is calling us to participate in the mission of God. According to the apostle Paul, it is the Spirit that comprehends the wisdom of God and therefore the Spirit that reveals this wisdom to us (1 Cor 2:9–10). Alternatively, those who are unspiritual, those without the mind of Christ, are unable to discern this wisdom of God (1 Cor 2:14). So, read the Bible on a regular basis just to hear God's word as a spiritual discipline.

With that in mind, this chapter discusses how a narrative reading of the Bible goes from a story on paper to the story we are living. It's a hermeneutic of discernment as we are being formed in the way of Christ.[1] It's the occasion or time *(kairos)* when God opens new space to walk forward on mission with God as local churches within our local communities.

The Missional Hermeneutic: Discerning the Work of God and Our Participation

Knowing that our participation in the mission of God is as much of a contextual endeavor as it is faithfully following Jesus, our reading of the Bible is never so banal and elementary as just repeating what we read. That approach may sound simple, but it's impossible and only creates further problems. Because the Bible is a collection of different contextual writings, discernment requires more nuance than just reading Scripture as though there is a one-to-one parallel between then and now.

---

1. Barton, *Pursuing God's Will Together*, 38, "Groups determined to pursue God's will together must begin by focusing on the dynamic of spiritual transformation in the lives of individuals who compromise the group. The temptation, of course, is to skip the necessary rework and get on with the business of discernment. No doubt some groups will try to do this. Not to worry; some lessons are best learned the hard way."

Living Gospel

Aware of the contextual differences between then and now, many readers understand that reading the Bible requires exegesis and consideration of Christian tradition. So, we turn to the Bible, often with the help of commentaries and other literary resources, to engage in a historical-grammatical exegesis and to familiarize ourselves with how others have understood the text. There is nothing inherently wrong with such a study of the Bible, as understanding the original intent of the writers of Scripture does matter. Likewise, knowing something about how other Christians throughout history have understood the Bible is also helpful. However, discerning our participation in the mission of God must raise other questions besides the exegetical questions we ask of Scripture.

Discernment certainly requires hearing what the scriptures teach and how the Christian Faith has been understood and practiced throughout history. However, since the contexts we live among are not parallel to those within Scripture, impetuously doing what was done in Scripture is neither wise nor always the right response. At this point, we should also remember that the Christian tradition is not monolithic. Yes, the Christian tradition has a lot to teach us. We can learn a lot from people like Augustine of Hippo and John Chrysostom to John Calvin and Jacob Arminius as well as the more contemporary voices like Dietrich Bonhoeffer and Martin Luther King Jr. Yet as we give them their rightful attention, we still must remember that they speak within their own cultural contexts.

So, besides understanding what the scriptures meant to their original recipients, as much as that is possible, and how the Christian tradition has understood the scriptures, discernment here is asking another question. The question has to do with how we are to embody the gospel, as it is revealed in Scripture, in a manner that is both faithful to Jesus and contextually apropos. In other words, *how do we bear witness as a living reflection of the gospel in a credible and legible manner today wherever God has placed us?* Answering this question requires a theological interpretation of Scripture that engages our understanding of what was said and done within Scripture for the bearing upon our own circumstances.[2]

---

2. The phrase "theological reading" is used by Volf, *Captive to the Word of God*, 16, who says "The Bible is therefore appropriately read as a narration of happenings, with an aim to understand what took place then and there and how what too place then and there was understood. A theological reading will do more than that; it will also attend to what bearing these past happenings have on what needs to happen here and now." Similarly, the phrase "theological hermeneutic" is used by Hicks, *Searching for the Pattern*, 112, who says, "Specifically, *we read the Bible to learn the heart, nature, and work of God, Jesus,*

Part Three: A Missional Reading of Scripture

This is where we go back to the Bible as a narrative, bringing Scripture into conversation with tradition and culture. Within this conversation is the realm of discernment, resulting in a *missional hermeneutic*. Now we have a lens through which we are able to begin discerning what our embodiment of the gospel will require. By bringing Scripture, tradition, and culture into a conversation, we are in a place where we can understand how God is working among us and the obedient response that the work of God requires of us. So, the conversation, our discernment, is both theological and practical, opening space for theological praxis—our embodiment of the gospel within our local contexts. It's also important at this point to remember that the Bible is a Christ-centered and Kingdom-oriented narrative.

Having a new set of eyes and ears to see and hear the work of God, we are encountering this God work within the Bible, Christian tradition, and culture. As our discernment progresses into actual participation, we understand that we are called to reflect what will at times be a very peculiar way of life. So, our missional hermeneutic is a lens that shapes our beliefs, values, and behaviors as an ethic that portrays the future, the new creation Jesus has inaugurated through his crucifixion, resurrection, and ascension.

As we read the Bible, whether from the Old or New Testament, we are invited to read in a manner that instructs us on how we follow Jesus and embody the kingdom of God he proclaimed. For example, in Deuteronomy 24:19–22, we read instructions about leaving a portion of the harvest for the aliens, orphans, and widows. Then in 1 Timothy 5:3–12, we read instructions regarding care for the widows. Taking both texts seriously does not necessitate that each set of instructions are obeyed in the same exact manner. Rather, what we see is God's concern for people who live with certain socio-economic disadvantages and his mercy enacted through tangible action carried out by his people. What each biblical text might ask of us is to take notice of the people around us who also live with socio-economic disadvantages, so that we might show the mercy of God through tangible actions ourselves.

As we embody the gospel within our local communities, how we do that will differ at times from not just one local church to another but from what we read in the Bible. What matters is not a uniform reduplication but that our embodiment of the gospel is both coherent with Jesus Christ

and the Holy Spirit. This provides guidance, wisdom, and direction for the people of God who want to imitate Jesus, the Son of God, in their lives and congregations through the strength of the Holy Spirit. This guidance, wisdom, and direction is based on God's identity, heart, and might acts."

and the kingdom of God as well as apropos to the circumstances at hand. That is what a faithful but contextual, or credible and legible, embodiment of the gospel is. And don't overthink this. No matter how much we tell ourselves otherwise, neither God nor our neighbors are fooled with poor, if not illegitimate, reflections of God. The duck test says, "If it smells like a duck, walks like a duck, etc . . . ." People, and especially God, can easily see the difference between the cruciform power of Christ that seeks to self-sacrificially serve others rather than the coercive power that is routinely on display among the world. A cursory reading of Scripture is sufficient to begin discerning whether our reflection of the gospel corresponds to Jesus Christ and the kingdom of God or whether we have adopted a utilitarian approach either for reasons of pragmatism or just because following Jesus just doesn't seem safe and prudent.

For this reason, discernment will often be an invitation to repentance. Richard Peace explains repentance as "a decision to change one's mind about God and the work of God. It involves new understanding and the ability and willingness to act upon this new understanding. Repentance means to turn away from the old understanding about God and to embrace the new understanding."[3] As we learn to follow Jesus and embody the gospel, we will encounter the challenge to let go of old habits, our old ways of thinking and doing, embracing instead the beliefs, values, and practices of God's kingdom revealed by Jesus.

Early on in his ministry, Jesus began encountering resistance as his embodiment of the gospel went against what others expected the kingdom of God to be. In response, Jesus told a quick parable about clothing and wineskins which we can read in Mark 2:21–22:

> "No one sews a piece of unshrunk cloth on an old cloak; otherwise, the patch pulls away from it, the new from the old, and a worse tear is made. And no one puts new wine into old wineskins; otherwise, the wine will burst the skins, and the wine is lost, and so are the skins; but one puts new wine into fresh wineskins."

This is why repentance, letting go of the old for the new that Jesus calls us to follow him in living, matters. It also matters as we read the Bible theologically. Our missional hermeneutic gives us the eyes to see the narrative of Scripture as the script we enact as followers of Jesus. Rather than just applying the Bible in a manner that is compatible with the lives we are already

---

3. Peace, *Conversion in the New Testament*, 251.

living, we let go of the old wineskins that are our lives. In letting go of the old, God may now pour the new wine of the gospel into the new wineskins so that the wine may ferment and age into a tasteful wine that others will want to drink from.

In pouring the new wine of the gospel upon us, God is opening space for us to consider what our discernment might become in practice. Ultimately, though, such discernment matters to the extent that we act upon our discernment. To both *hear* and *obey* are essential if we are to participate in the mission of God. So, there is an underlying question as we discern that we must always ask: *If we take Scripture seriously, then what about us must change?* Hearing and obeying, doing what we have discerned to be true in accordance with the good news of Jesus and the kingdom of God, is how we become performers of the story we are living.

Performance Time: Actors of the Story We Are Living

I'm a pastor, not an actor, and I surely don't want to insult the very lovely gift of the performing arts that acting graces society with. But I did act in a small play once during high school. It was a requirement for a class I enrolled in called Interpretive Acting or something along that line. One of the lessons I learned was that Broadway and Hollywood were most likely not in my future. All joking aside, I did learn something from that class. I remember how the teacher had us learning the characters within a particular story. We then were given a script, but instead of merely following the script line by line, we had to improvise.

Improvisation involves somewhat of a spontaneous performance within the present, the here and now, that responds to what else is happening. On stage, it's sort of an *ad hoc* production with rhyme and reason that tells a story. That is to say, good improvisation makes sense to those watching and listening to the performance.

So, it is with the gospel. Seeking a credible and legible embodiment of the gospel requires some improvisation. That, of course, requires learning to follow Jesus and entering into the kingdom of God from within the scriptures—the Bible as our script. Receiving the gospel as it is told within the Bible, we are invited to become actors within the story it tells—a story that includes the church community entrusted with the gospel, the cruciform rationale of the gospel, and the new creation that emerges from the

Living Gospel

gospel.[4] However, we can't misunderstand what improvisation means for embodying the gospel. We are not called to act as pretenders in which we are just portraying a character that is different from who we really are. As the church, we are the body of Christ, so we are playing ourselves within the story of the Bible. Our performance, the part we play within the story, must remain coherent with the story the Bible is telling because the part we are playing is really who we are. That is how our performance remains credible, while the legibility comes from our improvisation.

Similarly, improvisation does not mean we are just making things up as we go along. Although there is not an absolute, sure-proof insured way of avoiding such fictionality, we avoid such absurdities by continuing to read the Bible again and again. This enables us to gain more and more familiarity with the story the Bible is telling. In doing so, we become aware of how the story has unfolded and where it is going as a complete and coherent narrative. Improvisation, then, becomes the function necessitating the discernment of what we must do and how such a task should be expressed.

N.T. Wright suggests that one way of discerning our participation is to imagine ourselves as actors within the storyline.[5] As local churches reading the Bible, we are encountering the particular details of a text, along with its teachings and instructions, taking note of where the text is located within the storyline. Then, bringing the scripture into conversation with Christian tradition and the cultural context we inhabit, we are able to reimagine how we are called to a *faithful improvisation* as followers of Jesus. What makes this enactment both faithful and improvisation is that we are neither repeating the past for the sake of repetition nor are we acting contrary to the confessional life of the church within the Bible and Christian tradition.

Our faithfulness yields a continuity with the storyline so that our performance makes sense with the story Scripture tells, while our improvisation avoids the redundancy that over time loses meaning as our local contexts change. Think of our performance as acting within a five-act play,

---

4. Hays, *The Moral Vision of the New Testament*, 196, offers the three images of community, cross, and new creation that help guide our reading of scripture as well as how we preform these interpretations. The image of community takes into account how scripture addresses our embodiment of the gospel as a community. The cross offers the rationale in guiding the characteristic of our performance. Lastly, the image of new creation is a reminder that our performance is to be a proleptic witness of the redemptive future—though unfinished as it is—among the present.

5. The following model for reading scripture is indebted to Wright, *Scripture and the Authority of God*, 121–27;—-, *The New Testament and the People of God*, 139–43.

Part Three: A Missional Reading of Scripture

as N.T. Wright has described, in which the church locates its place in the storyline as part of the fifth and final act. The caveat is recognizing that even though the New Testament provides the first scenes of the fifth act and some glimpses of the final scene in this final act, the scenes that churches today are scheduled to perform are missing. What are we to do? Doing what was done before, line by line in the same exact manner, seems more like a live-streamed video that freezes. But if our improvisation resembles characters like the might-makes-right machoism found in the action-movie genre or the angry winner-takes-all mentality that has become American politics, to use but two examples, then it's no longer the gospel we are embodying.

Far from doing whatever we want, our improvisation always seeks to remain a consistent and truthful portrayal of the gospel itself while always translating the gospel locally. This evokes a certain tension between coherency and contextualization that will always, or should always, be with us. However, that's because just as we are restricted from doing whatever we want, we must also avoid mere repetition of the past.

Another way of understanding our performance is to think of ourselves as playing in a jazz ensemble. As any musician knows, playing in a jazz ensemble requires a lot of improvisation. The music itself prescribes the key, time signature, rhythm, and chord progression, which the performer must stay within for the improvised playing to remain continuous and coherent with the musical piece and the rest of the band. However, if the musician just persisted in repeatedly playing the same notes of a previous measure—whether the first measure, the sixteenth measure, or even the twenty-first measure—the music would become awkwardly redundant and lose any sense of meaning. Though some repetitions with a little nuance may be necessary, such as repeating the chorus, the musicians understand that their performance must be more than just repetition. Now imagine the local church performing the jazz ensemble with the narrative of Scripture music providing the key, time signature, rhythm, and chord progression. In this sense, the story the Bible tells does set some limits on the sort of improvisation that is allowed. However, within the storyline is the freedom to improvise in a Christ-centered manner that carries the story forward toward its Kingdom-oriented goal.[6]

---

6. Wright, *Scripture and the Authority of God*, 121–27. I might add that, as anyone who has ever played music already understands, it is very obvious when a musician is performing in the wrong key, in the wrong tempo, etc. . . . If it were not for the sinful human propensity of self-deception, it too would be very obvious when a church is no longer performing the Christ-Centered and Kingdom-Oriented script.

Conclusion

Some might wonder about the subjective nature of this conversation, but is there any pure objective hermeneutical lens? All interpretation of the Bible is done by fallible humans who read Scripture as well as reflect upon tradition and culture while embedded within their own particular lenses. Though we can do ourselves a great favor by becoming aware of the lenses we see through and how they shape our vision, a total pure vision is impossible.[7] It is always possible that our discerned actions, based on the conclusions we draw in the missional conversation, will be wrong, which is why our discernment must be an ongoing community endeavor. While a community of believers discerning together doesn't guarantee anything, we must have faith that God is at work and therefore trust the Spirit to lead the community in discernment.

More importantly, though, we must act on that faith. Our faith is always an embodied faith, both a confession and practice. That is our proclamation of the gospel, in word and deed. Our embodiment of the gospel and our participation in the mission of God will always contain an element of weakness and imperfection. This is not an acceptance of mediocrity but an acknowledgment of our humanity which God has chosen to work through. Therefore, we trust that God will bring about his good through our faithfulness as we follow Jesus, embodying a credible and legible portrait of the gospel.

---

7. To understand more why this objectivity is impossible, which has to do with the link between modernism and postmodernism, see Toulmin, *Cosmopolis*, 179.

Part Four

Christ-Formed and Spirit-Filled

9

The Christ-Formed Church
Reclaiming Our Identity as Kingdom Citizens

"Know, first, who you are, and then adorn yourself accordingly."
—EPICTETUS

EVERYTHING WRITTEN THUS FAR is premised on the conviction that an embodiment of the gospel among local churches must always be contextualized. Therefore, while similarities from one church to another will always exist, there will also be differences because of the differing contexts. So, it is with a certain hesitation that I attempt to demonstrate how this missional hermeneutic works. There are many questions facing local churches that neither I nor anyone else can answer apart from participating in the life of each local church and its local community.

Consider how the practice of justice and reconciliation for a church located in the city of Memphis might differ from a church in Tucson, Arizona, or Montpelier, Vermont. Yes, there are some core tenets of the gospel that are essential regardless of context, but any contextualized theological praxis will depend also on the different contexts.

For this reason, it is rather presumptuous and impetuous to suggest what the missional hermeneutic discussed in this book means for any number of issues facing local churches. Yet there are some challenges facing Christianity in America, regardless of context, denomination, etc. . . .

Part Four: Christ-Formed and Spirit-Filled

In this chapter and the next, I will discuss two issues for the purpose of demonstrating how Christians might employ the missional hermeneutic toward the theological praxis of the church.

We Always Go Back to Our Story

As followers of Jesus, God has formed us together as a community called the church, and so we must ask ourselves what exactly this means. Hans Urs von Balthasar reminds us that the church is not to be a closed community preoccupied with its affairs. Quite the opposite—the church is tasked with "communicating to the rest of mankind the universally valid truths concerning God's liberating and redeeming work with fundamental openness, which in itself is but the continuation of God's involvement in Christ for the sake of the world."[1] Such a task is more than just evangelism, church planting, and making disciples; it gets to the core of our identity in Christ.

When we reflect systematically upon ecclesiology, the Christian doctrine of the church, it's typically to give a lot of attention to the identity of the church by noting the identifying markers and core practices of the church. This includes doctrines like Christ as the head of the church and the priesthood of all believers as well as practices like baptism and the Lord's Supper. All of this is appropriate, but here I want to limit reflection to the identity of the church as a people and what that involves as a theological praxis in terms of posture and engagement among the world.

When turning to the New Testament, we find the Apostle Paul describing Gentile Christians as now "no longer strangers and aliens, but you are citizens with the saints and also members of the household of God" (Eph 2:19). Rather than identifying these Gentiles as Roman citizens, Paul says they belong to a different kind of community. While he uses the imagery of a household, Paul views the community of people as belonging to God rather than any human authority. The apostle Peter similarly describes Christians as "a chosen race, a royal priesthood, a holy nation, God's own people . . ." who are then regarded as "aliens and exiles" (1 Pet 2:9, 11).

Most of us probably don't get up in the morning and think of ourselves as aliens and exiles because we are Christians. Such language seems sort of strange and indeed very strange to some. Several years ago, I was sitting in a Starbucks writing a sermon on 1 Peter 2. Out of curiosity, I decided to ask several random people sitting at the table next to me what

1. Balthasar, *Engagement With God*, 32.

The Christ-Formed Church

they might think of a church that described themselves as aliens and exiles. One person asked with a strange look on his face, "Why would a church say that?" The woman sitting across from him seemed even more perplexed when she asked, "Is that a cult or something?"

Intrigued by their responses, I also asked them what religious affiliation, if any, they claimed. Both respondents claimed to be Christians. I didn't ask for any more details, and there could be several reasons for their unfamiliarity with what I was inquiring about. Nevertheless, their responses reflect the peculiarity of this language. Yet, as strange as it might sound to our western ears, both Peter and Paul are speaking about the identity of Christians; there is a history with such language. For that, we must keep the entire narrative of Scripture in mind.

As we do so, let's begin by recalling how God liberated Israel from the tyranny of Egyptian oppression. Years of living in captivity shaped the way Israelites regarded themselves, as it would anyone. So, in electing Israel to be the people through whom the Lord would be known among the entire world, Moses reacquaints the Israelites with their true identity as people created in the image of God (Gen 1:26–27). That is an identity marker right there, signifying Israel as God's representative in the world.[2]

Within the story, as it unfolds, the identity of Israel is clarified even further. As the Lord is entering into covenant with Israel, the Lord instructs Moses to speak these words to the Israelites written in Exodus 19:5–6, "Now therefore, if you obey my voice and keep my covenant, *you shall be my treasured possession out of all the peoples. Indeed, the whole earth is mine, but you shall be for me a priestly kingdom and a holy nation.*" These words identify Israel as the people of God among the nations with a priestly purpose.

In our day, it's quite common to think of clergy people when we hear the word "priest." Whatever we might think of identifying clergy people as priests, the image can help us understand the function God is assigning to the identity of Israel. A priest is someone who stands between God and people as a go-between. The priest represents God to the people and the people to God. The priest speaks for God to the people, imparting his instruction and wisdom, but the priest also will act on behalf of the people toward God, such as praying or receiving confession.

As Israel is called to live in covenant with God, their lives are to serve in a priestly role among the rest of the nations. By keeping the Torah as they entered the promised land, they would reveal their wisdom to the other

---

2. Brueggemann, *Theology of the Old Testament*, 452.

people around them who in turn see the Lord at work among them (Deut 4:5–8). The problem is that Israel will forget to do as they are instructed, failing to live as the people God has redeemed them and is forming them to be.

The book of Joshua tells the story of Israel entering the promised land, but what should have been an eleven-day journey turned into a forty-year wandering because of their inability to listen and trust (Num 14:1–3, 10–11, 34; Deut 1:1–2). From the triumphalist proclamations of Israel saying they will serve the Lord at the end of Joshua, we turn to the book of Judges only to read one story after another of Israel doing evil and turning to idolatry.

Moving on through the Old Testament, we read in chapter 8 of 1 Samuel how Israel demanded that the prophet Samuel appoint them a king. Why would they want to do what the Lord viewed as a rejection of him? The people said to Samuel, "There must be a king over us so we can be like all the other nations" (vs. 19–20). Such an admission is revealing. In some sense, Israel has forgotten her own identity. Instead of serving as God's people, with the priestly role among the nations, Israel wants to be like the other nations.

This desire will have dire consequences that will eventually lead Israel deeper and deeper into idolatry and injustice. Israel became a divided nation, with the northern kingdom of Israel and the southern kingdom of Judah. Eventually, though, both kingdoms were conquered by the Babylonians and taken off into captivity, resulting in what we refer to as exile. Though Israel began to question whether God would ever forgive his people, God was faithful to the covenant he made and did extend his steadfast love and mercy to Israel.

For all the doom and gloom that people sometimes assume the prophets of Israel preached, they also proclaimed a message of messianic hope. One such prophet was Isaiah, who assured the people that God would comfort his people and that he would renew those who hope in him (40:1, 28–31) and would gather Israel as her savior (43:1–3). However, in the midst of this redemptive proclamation, Isaiah also told the people that Israel would again be the light to other nations (42:6, 49:6, 60:3), fulfilling their role as "priests of the Lord" and "ministers of our God" (61:6).

This is familiar language to Christians. This is what God has finally accomplished in Jesus Christ, who came into the Galilean region of Israel announcing the good news of God's kingdom with a call for people to repent, believe, and follow him (Matt 4:17, 19; Mark 1:15, 17). At this point in the history of Israel, there was still a feeling of living in exile since Israel

The Christ-Formed Church

remained under the rule of the Romans.[3] The question on the mind of many Jews was when God would restore the kingdom which was salvation for Israel. The answer to that question, to which all four Gospels uniquely answer, is that God was restoring the kingdom and making good on his redemptive promise in Jesus Christ and particularly through his crucifixion and resurrection.

The same question is also answered by the apostle Peter in Acts 2 with his Pentecost message. The occasion for the message is the outpouring of the Holy Spirit, which is the sign that God is restoring his kingdom. Recalling both the prophet Joel as well as several Psalms, Peter explains how God raised the crucified Jesus from death and exalted him as Lord and Messiah. Beyond this, Peter issues what my church tradition calls an invitation to repentance and baptism for all who want to participate in this restored kingdom.

What emerges is the birth, so to speak, of a new community that we now refer to as the church. As a baptized people, the church is to live under the authority (in the name) of Jesus by the power (gift) of the Holy Spirit. For in their baptism, the people have been crucified with Christ and therefore raised into a new life that exists in Christ (Rom 6:3–4; Gal 2:15–21).[4]

The New Testament further explains how the grace of God has gone from the redemption of one specific ethnicity to life for all, both Jews and Gentiles, to participate in. However, just as Israel was called to serve as a priestly role among the world, now the church takes up that same role. The community of the baptized are no longer regarded as citizens among this world but aliens and exiles belonging to a kingdom not of this world, living as the salt of the earth and light of the world Jesus declares his disciples to be (Matt 5:13–16). This new community is the church that God has raised up in Christ to carry forth his mission among the world.

Exiles Taking up Residence as Sojourners

Today it is quite common to hear Christians say that we are "to be in the world but not of the world." This phrase, which has become rather cliché is

---

3. Wright, *The New Testament and the People of God*, 269.

4. Gorman, *Inhabiting the Cruciform God*, 73–74. That Christian baptism is the means by which believers are crucified and raised into a new life in Christ is also the precise reason why the apostle Paul raises the question of baptism in Romans 6 in response to the question of whether the church should continue sinning. Baptism is an identity marker that signifies believers as no longer belonging to the old life (creation) of "Adam" but now belong to the new life (creation) of Christ.

based on words that Jesus prayed on the evening before he was crucified. According to John 14:17, Jesus says, "I have given them your word, and the world has hated them because they do not belong to the world, just as I do not belong to the world." So the exhortation to be in the world but not of the world is certainly appropriate but we must understand that it cannot be reduced to individual morality.

It is certainly good that the we who are Christians live a life that avoids greed, dishonesty, lust, and so forth. The world may live such lives but not those who profess the name of Christ, who have been set free from sin, and have been made a new creation in Christ. However, this difference must extend to our understanding of what it means to live as the church. We must recapture our identity as exiles, as that is part of what it means to be holy just as the Lord is holy (1 Pet 1:16).

For far too many years, Christians have separated living as the church from much of the public life. That wasn't always the case. Once upon a time Christians, as Gerald Sitter reminds us, "did not try to separate religious ritual and public conduct, as most ancient religions appeared to do. The Christian Faith mandated that all of one's life be submitted to God."[5] For Christians, allegiance was to King Jesus rather than any king or nation of this world. So Christian living meant a consistent and coherent way of life that reflected the existence of God's reign—the kingdom of God. To say it another way, Christians did not have one ethic for what we might call an individualistic and privatized religious life and another for the social-political public life, resulting in simultaneously trying to serve the ends (*telos*) of two different kingdoms.

Christian identity as the church was a holistic existence shaped by the in-breaking reign of God in Jesus, the Lord and Messiah. Of course, this meant that Christians were at odds with the society at large and as most people know, this resulted in various periods of persecution. Rather than rethinking their identity and presence in life, the church embraced their reality as exiles living in the world. Besides the New Testament descriptions of the church as foreigners living as sojourners or exiles (Jas 1:1; 1 Pet 1:1; 2:11), this is understanding common enough for other early Christian writings to speak of the church with exilic descriptions. For example, *First Clement* begins with "The church of God, living in exile in Roma, to the church of God, exiled in Corinth . . ."[6] Then in the early second century,

---

5. Sittser, *Water from a Deep Well*, 60.
6. Clement, *1 Clem*, 1.

the opening of the *Epistle of Polycarp* is "to the church of God that sojourns at Philippi . . ."[7]

One of the most fascinating descriptions of the exilic life the early church embodied is found in the late second-century writing called the *Epistle of Diognetus*. Christians are depicted as people who:

> . . . live in their own countries, but only as aliens. They have a share in everything as citizens, and endure everything as foreigners. Every foreign land is their fatherland, and yet for them every fatherland is a foreign land. They marry, like everyone else, and they beget children, but they do not cast out their offspring. They share their bread with each other, but not their marriage bed. It is true that they are "in the flesh," but they do not live "according to the flesh."[8]

Here we are reminded that in one sense, the early Christians were typical people like everyone else. They worked and did business in the market places just as others, with many of them, marrying and growing as families just like people of all cultures do. Yet even though the Roman empire counted them as citizens, Christians regarded themselves as foreigners taking up residence as a sojourner. They understood that rather than participating in the Roman empire, seeking to make it a great nation or kingdom, they were now participants in the mission of God belonging to the kingdom of God. As the apostle Paul once said, they were now citizens of heaven (Phil 3:20) and their entire life was lived for the purpose of bearing witness to the good news of Jesus Christ and the kingdom of God that was now already at hand.

Reclaiming Our Identity as the Church

Christians today must learn to recapture this understanding of Christianity, with its peculiar identity and purpose. When we read Scripture as participants in the mission of God, we understand that we are called to follow Jesus in living our lives under the reign of God. More than just saying we belong to the kingdom of God, that we've received the forgiveness of sins, and that we're going to be with Jesus once our physical bodies die, we are called by Jesus to live solely for the purpose of God's kingdom just as Jesus

---

7. Polycarp, *To the* Philippians, 1.
8. *Letter to Diognetus*, 5.

Part Four: Christ-Formed and Spirit-Filled

did. To do any less is to divorce discipleship from the grace of God, which results in what Dietrich Bonhoeffer regarded as cheap grace.[9]

Only to the degree that we recapture this understanding of Christianity will we truly live as participants in the mission of God. This is our call from Jesus to repentance, to stop living for the causes that are not of the kingdom, and to believe that the kingdom of God has come so that we may follow Jesus as a witness to this very truth.[10] This is not a call to ignore the problems that plague society. Just as Jesus lived a life that extended mercy and sought justice/righteousness amidst great suffering and terrible injustices, so must the church do so from an imagination formed in the way of Christ rather than partisan politics. The evils of racism, the well-being of the unborn, the care for the poor, the concern for victims of human trafficking, to name a few matters germane to the twenty-first century in America, all matter much and should be of concern for those who dare claim to follow Jesus. However, we must remember that our resources for addressing such matters derive from the gospel, not conservative and liberal ideologies that are trending today (though we can certainly learn from resources in the vast fields of the humanities and sciences).

This is a point that cannot be stressed enough. When Christians sound like good spokespeople for conservative and liberal politics in America and spend endless hours trying to bring about the partisan outcomes of these ideologies, the church begins to look like a bunch of elephants and donkeys rather than the crucified Christ who is head of the church. As Christians, we are called to be "partisans of Christ, people who advocate the cause of Christ, people who even play the part, acting like Christ."[11] It is hard to imagine how that is possible when Christians seem more interested in playing the role of partisan politics.

Pastors should take note too. The attention we are given to speak into the lives of those we have been called to serve is diminishing and distracted by many other voices whose aims are not the gospel. Notwithstanding the ethical issues of using the pulpit as a partisan political platform, it would

---

9. Bonhoeffer, *The Cost of Discipleship*, 44–45 (page citation is to the reprint edition), not only describes what he considers to be cheap grace but compares it to what he describes as costly grace.

10. Camp, *Scandalous Witness*, 25, "Christian discipleship calls us to a proleptic stance in which we embody and bear witness to the world that is coming. We labor *now*, plowing and sowing and watering and reaping the varied firstfruits of that still-coming kingdom."

11. Vanhoozer, *Faith Speaking Understanding*, 114.

be a shame to waste the attention we are given not just telling Christians whether they should vote or not but who they should vote for.

I can remember being a fly on the wall in a coffee shop listening in on a conversation that another local pastor was having with two women. For nearly an hour, the pastor talked, sometimes almost ranting, in order to persuade these two women who they should vote for in an upcoming presidential election. As the conversation continued, one of the women began to look frustrated. After the conversation was over and the pastor left, the lady who was frustrated looked at the other lady and said, "For crying out loud, he's a pastor, and all he wants to do is tell me why I should vote for . . ." As I sat there, I couldn't help but think how much of a wasted opportunity that was.

Among an increasingly post-Christian society, the church cannot continue wasting its voice on things that at best will be a tiny footnote in the annals of history. What matters is the gospel of Jesus Christ, full stop.

This point is not to dismiss the necessary role that politics play in maintaining a civil society where life can ideally flourish for all people. Despite the problems we see, we should be thankful for every civil servant and elected official, and we ought to pray for them, for we all reap the good they do in their work. Nor is my point to suggest whether or not Christians should vote in civil elections. However, we need to remember that there is a difference between praying for the governing officials and participating in the kingdoms they serve. We would even do ourselves a favor if we would recall more often the exhortation in the *Apocalypse of Jesus Christ* regarding Babylon, "Come out of her, my people, so that you do not take part in her sins, and so that you do not share in her plagues" (Rev 18:4). Besides, as Lee C. Camp whimsically puts it, "hostile and belligerent partisanship among American Christians might be compared to a fistfight over table manners on the sinking *Titanic*."[12]

As we seek to reclaim our true identity as the church, we must remember the character of our participation in the mission of God. Our posture is not one of coercion that seeks to impose the will of God—not by legislation and certainly not by the sword. We are called to follow the self-sacrificial servanthood way of Christ as a witness to the in-breaking kingdom of God and that is always contingent upon our means reflecting the way of Christ. It is the gospel, understood from a Christ-centered and Kingdom-oriented reading of Scripture, that must form our theological praxis. This is what

---

12. Camp, *Scandalous Witness*, 100.

it means to be the church among our world, to be citizens *among* society taking up residence as aliens and exiles as God's chosen priesthood.

Although reclaiming this posture can never guarantee that we will endear ourselves to the rest of society, there are people, seekers as we often call them, who might begin to catch a glimpse of God's kingdom. Our life as the church will become a living explanation of what God has accomplished in Jesus Christ and what that means for the future. In other words, we once again reclaim our proleptic witness to the new creation that is already present but not yet fully revealed. This means our task as the church is the function of what Irwyn Ince Jr. describes as a "forward-facing mirror" in which others will catch "a glimpse of where the world is heading."[13]

Conclusion

Reading the Bible as the story that we are living as followers of Jesus allows us to see how God has called his people of the past to join in his work. Rather than reading the Bible as a disjointed text, we can see that a part of God's mission has always included the formation of a people who would participate in his mission. We also know the goal of this mission is fulfilled in Jesus Christ, particularly through his crucifixion, resurrection, and exaltation.

Our reading of Scripture, with our awareness of the entire biblical narrative, also allows us to understand truly what it means to be the church living on mission with God. The aim of this chapter was to demonstrate how the missional hermeneutic articulated in this book begins to shape our ecclesiology, specifically. There are certainly many other questions we will wonder about—some we might easily find answers to, and others will be more difficult. One of these questions pertains to how the Holy Spirit gifts us as a church to live on mission with God. That is the question we now turn our attention to.

---

13. Ince Jr., *The Beautiful Community*, 113.

10

The Spirit-Filled Church

All People Blessed to Bless All People

> "Stop asking God to bless what you're doing. Find
> out what God's doing. It's already blessed."
>
> —BONO

ON THE WAY TO my office one recent morning, I received a text. So, while stopped at a red light, I quickly read the text. It was from one of the shepherds of our church notifying myself and several others that another person had brought a bunch of extra groceries to the church building for anyone in need of extra food.

It wasn't more than fifteen minutes when another person notified us that she would be picking up some of those groceries and delivering them to a couple of families in need.

"What an example of mercy in the name of Jesus," I thought. I know both of these people work full-time jobs and have other responsibilities, but that doesn't prevent them from serving as God has gifted them to do so through his Spirit. In fact, not even COVID-19 has hindered such serving.

Serving is what the church does when the church is right. Baptized in the name of Jesus Christ and having received the Spirit, the church embodies the gospel as a witness to the kingdom-reign of God. Such embodiment is participation in the mission of God. It is living as God's work of art displaying the new creation that God is bringing about in Christ. It is, in a nutshell, serving.

The Christian Good

The Drop Box was a documentary film released in 2015. The film tells the work of pastor Lee Jon Rak and his wife Chun-ja, who serve with the Jusarang Community Church in Seoul, South Korea, where they care for abandoned children. Mothers, many of them young and single and sometimes victims of sexual violence, are unable to care for their babies and so they place the children in a "drop box" where the pastor and his wife receive these children.

With a sign placed outside by the box that reads "place to leave babies," hundreds of children have been rescued and cared for. Pastor Lee Jon estimates receiving around two hundred and fifty babies every year.

Some stories of love make the headlines and rightfully so, but not all do. As I think about this wonderful ministry in Seoul, I also think of another lady named Maud. She was a Christian who was a member of a little country church, the first church I ever preached for, in Hardy, Arkansas.

Vocationally, Maud had served as a public educator for nearly fifty years in the state of Arkansas before retiring. When she started teaching in the 1930s, up in the Ozark Mountains, rural poverty was all around. There were few secondary educational opportunities available, and so many children did not receive any education beyond elementary school. However, understanding the need for education, Maud not only taught in the elementary school, but she also began voluntarily teaching secondary education to children.

Both stories are examples of Christians using their talents and opportunities to serve as a blessing to others. Also, both stories bear witness in different ways to the kingdom of God. The point, however, is not to suggest that only Christians are capable of love and doing such good. We only need to open our eyes a little every day to see examples—sometimes big but many times very low-key—of non-Christians doing good. Years ago, as a novice driver, I was in a terrific auto accident that required an eight-hour facial reconstructive surgery. After the car insurance paid their portion of the medical bills, my parents were still left with a significant bill for my surgery. However, the Muslim surgeon, Dr. Arab, who was not only a skilled physician but also a generous man, waived the rest of the bill for my parents.

The Spirit-Filled Church

Certainly, and regardless of religion or even politics, for that matter, people are capable of doing all sorts of good, acting with love for others just like God created us to live. That's part of what it means to bear the image of God. It is to live in such a way as to be a blessing to others for the flourishing of life just as God has blessed our life to flourish.[1] Regardless of the sin—which is sometimes awfully evil—that all people are capable of, every person is created in the image of God. As cataclysmic as sin is to our lives and the story we are living, the reality of sin has not changed the fact that all people still bear the divine image of the Creator (Gen 1:26–27, 5:1).

What sets Christians apart is not the fact that we bless others or even how we bless others. Rather, it is our reason that distinguishes us and the good works we do. To be a Christian means living as followers of Jesus filled with the Holy Spirit and therefore serving among the world as God's people bearing witness to the kingdom of God. That's our task as the church and what it means to participate in the mission of God. As Leonard Allen says, "In the power of the Spirit, the church is God's contrast society, an alternative community modeling a new humanity and called to be 'a light to the nations.'"[2] Our good works, the ways in which we bless others, are done because we understand that this is how God created life to be lived and how life is lived in the coming new creation in Christ that we now partake of. The mission of God we participate in is to proclaim this new creation, the kingdom of God, as the life God is cultivating and now invites all people to join. We simply live this life of blessing because that is how we really ought to live.

The Empowering Work of the Spirit

How then shall we bless others? At face value, this seems like an easy question to answer. Surely, we will bless others as we learn to follow Jesus. When we consider the Holy Spirit, we may think of the fruit of the Spirit—love, joy,

---

1. Bauckham, *Bible and Mission*, 34, "Blessing in the Bible refers to God's characteristically generous and abundant giving of all good to his creatures and his continual renewal of the abundance of created life. Blessing is God's provision for human flourishing. But it is also relational: to be blessed by God is not only to know God's good gifts but to know God himself in his generous giving. Because it is relational: the movement of blessing is a movement that goes out from God and returns to him. God's blessing of people overflows in their blessing of others and those who experience blessing from God in turn bless God, which means that they give all that creatures really can give to God: thanksgiving and praise."

2. Allen, *Poured Out*, 173–74.

Part Four: Christ-Formed and Spirit-Filled

peace, patience, kindness, goodness, faithfulness, gentleness, and self-control (Gal 5:22–23)—knowing that such fruit will bless others in various ways.

However, we also belong to the church, both as the universal body of Christ and a local community of believers. It is wonderful when individuals do good works, but how do we do so joined together as the church? How do we serve within our church as well as the community we live among and beyond? Answering these questions requires giving our attention to the work of the Holy Spirit among us.

We know from reading Scripture that the restoration of the kingdom came with the outpouring of the Holy Spirit. On the Day of Pentecost in Acts 2, Peter quoted from the prophet Joel, saying in vs. 17–18:

> In the last days it will be, God declares, that I will pour out my Spirit upon all flesh, and your sons and your daughters shall prophesy, and your young men shall see visions, and your old men shall dream dreams. Even upon my slaves, both men and women, in those days I will pour out my Spirit; and they shall prophesy.

We will come back to this passage later in this chapter, but for now, we need to recognize the importance of this fulfillment of prophesy. At the end of the message, the summons to repent and be baptized came with the promised gift of the Holy Spirit (v. 38). God has now given the same Spirit that descended upon Jesus in his baptism (Matt 3:16; Mark 1:10; Luke 2:21–22) to the people, the church, who will live in the name of Jesus as they continue the work of Jesus. So, the Spirit is the animating power by which the church goes forth on mission with God.

Many rightfully wonder what it looks like for the church to live by the power of the Holy Spirit. My own church tradition has historically often neglected the work of the Holy Spirit while viewing with suspicion some of the claims other denominations have made regarding the work of the Spirit among the church. Consequently, talking about the work of the Holy Spirit creates some tension. I understand, but I also want to caution us at this point. Though the Spirit dwells among us, we don't own the Spirit. Remember, we don't control God, and therefore we should not attempt to control, mange, etc. the Spirit of God.

What we believe is that the Spirit of God is the third person of the Trinity. As Christians, we worship the One Triune God who exists in three persons: Father, Son, and Spirit. The unity or oneness of God means the work of the Spirit is the work of God the Father and the Son. Therefore, the Spirit will always lead us to live according to the will of God the Father revealed in the Son. Though there is much room for discussion as to what exactly the will of God entails, we do believe the will of God is revealed by Jesus and is understood particularly through Scripture. So, while there will always be some disagreement among Christians on any given point, we can know God and his will. In fact, we know who God is because we know Jesus who "is the reflection of God's glory and the exact imprint of God's very being . . ." (Heb 1:3). Jesus Christ is the reflection of who God really is, and the Spirit is forming us so that the character of God revealed in Jesus Christ becomes our character.[3]

"Therefore be imitators of God . . . ," says the apostle Paul (Eph 5:1). In the formation of our character, the Spirit empowers us to live as the artwork of God. Empowered by the same Spirit that led Jesus to live in submission to his Father, the Spirit forms us to carry forth as participants in the same mission Jesus participated within. So, the Spirit will never lead us to speak or act in ways incoherent with the life and character of Jesus. Instead, the Spirit empowers us to live, by faith, as followers of Jesus who are empowered to serve in various ways as a local church to the glory of God.

This is where the language of spiritual gifts comes from, which is based on the New Testament word *charisma* (pl. *charismata*). Charisma refers to various talents and abilities that God has given the church from his Spirit as "gifts of grace springing from the creative grace of God."[4] We only have to read the way Luke describes the life of the believers to see how God gifts his people to embody the gospel in some extraordinary ways (Acts 2:42–47, 4:32–37). When the mission became too much for the twelve apostles to manage on their own, God revealed seven other men he had gifted with the talent for managing the daily distribution of food (Acts 6:1–7).

The believers were not trying to fit some predetermined form or pattern of what the church should look like to outside observers. Likewise, they were not trying to establish any kind of pattern. They were simply seeking to embody the gospel, to live under the authority of Jesus Christ by the power of the Holy Spirit, as a witness to the kingdom-reign of God. Out of their faith in what God had accomplished in Jesus Christ, the believers

---

3. Powell, Hicks, and McKinzie, *Discipleship in Community*, 80, "The creative goodness, majestic power, faithful loving-kindness, and compassionate justice of the Lord become palpable, tangible, and shockingly intimate in the incarnate Word, full of grace and truth. The Father through the Son pours out the Spirit on the messianic people, and God's character becomes their character . . ."

4. Moltmann, *The Church in the Power of the Spirit*, 295.

Part Four: Christ-Formed and Spirit-Filled

were simply opening themselves to the Spirit so that they would serve as a living testimony to the gospel.

Although God appointed some to be apostles or missionaries, not all believers were to fulfill such a role. In Scripture, we are told "some would be apostles, some prophets, some evangelists, some pastors and teachers, to equip the saints for the work of ministry, for building up the body of Christ..." (Eph 4:11–12). But there are other ways in which the Spirit has empowered different believers to serve among the church as participants in the mission of God. There are three particular passages of Scripture that describe different ways God gifts his people:

> *Romans 12:4–8:* "For as in one body we have many members, and not all the members have the same function, so we, who are many, are one body in Christ, and individually we are members one of another. We have gifts that differ according to the grace given to us: prophecy, in proportion to faith; ministry, in ministering; the teacher, in teaching; the exhorter, in exhortation; the giver, in generosity; the leader, in diligence; the compassionate, in cheerfulness."

> *1 Corinthians 12:1–11:* "Now concerning spiritual gifts, brothers and sisters, I do not want you to be uninformed. You know that when you were pagans, you were enticed and led astray to idols that could not speak. Therefore I want you to understand that no one speaking by the Spirit of God ever says "Let Jesus be cursed!" and no one can say "Jesus is Lord" except by the Holy Spirit. Now there are varieties of gifts, but the same Spirit; and there are varieties of services, but the same Lord; and there are varieties of activities, but it is the same God who activates all of them in everyone. To each is given the manifestation of the Spirit for the common good. To one is given through the Spirit the utterance of wisdom, and to another the utterance of knowledge according to the same Spirit, to another faith by the same Spirit, to another gifts of healing by the one Spirit, to another the working of miracles, to another prophecy, to another the discernment of spirits, to another various kinds of tongues, to another the interpretation of tongues. All these are activated by one and the same Spirit, who allots to each one individually just as the Spirit chooses."

> *1 Peter 4:10–11:* "Like good stewards of the manifold grace of God, serve one another with whatever gift each of you has received. Whoever speaks must do so as one speaking the very words of God; whoever serves must do so with the strength that God supplies, so

> that God may be glorified in all things through Jesus Christ. To him belong the glory and the power forever and ever. Amen."

Although the three passages are listed here in order of their canonical appearance in the Bible, the point is not to create one single inventory of spiritual gifts. Space will not permit any discussion regarding the differences in the three passages of Scripture or what each particular gift mentioned entails. Furthermore, there doesn't seem to be any reason to say that every local church will receive all of the above-mentioned gifts or that the way in which the Spirit gifts the different people within the church is limited to what is mentioned in these passages.

The point here is to recognize that the Spirit empowers every believer to serve so that the church as a collective body displays itself as the artwork of God. However God forms these talents and abilities in us, we are equipped for good works. Because these gifts are animated by the Spirit, we are equipped for works that we will never accomplish relying on our own human power. That doesn't mean that every good work will manifest in a radical and extraordinary manner. Sometimes such good works will be as mundane as those widows who were "bringing up children, showing hospitality, washing the feet of the Lord's people, helping those in trouble and devoting herself to all kinds of good deeds" (1 Tim 5:10).

What makes our good works spiritual, that is of the Spirit and therefore empowered by the Spirit, flows from the obedient faith we live by in the name of Jesus Christ. As we discern God at work opening space for us to serve, we trust God by using our talents and gifts as followers of Jesus. We serve like this even when doing so is inconvenient, risky, and even means doing something that we may not completely understand at the moment (and so not allowing common sense or conventional wisdom to impede the work of the Spirit). Such trust and obedience to God is our faith, lived in reliance upon the Spirit rather than ourselves. As a result, our embodiment of the gospel is formed not just by our understanding of Scripture, tradition, and culture but also by the Spirit-given gifts and talents we have received.

Open for Every Believer?

Up to this point, we have observed how the Spirit enables the church to participate in the mission of God as followers of Jesus. Every local church, then, is a community of redeemed and reconciled believers who exists under the authority of Jesus Christ by the power of the Spirit. This is the gospel

Part Four: Christ-Formed and Spirit-Filled

blessing from God. It is grace received and therefore grace which the Spirit enables the church to extend as a blessing to each other and their neighbors at large—the local community and beyond.

However, for the church to extend the blessing of God, the church must allow space for every believer to serve as they have been gifted. Admittedly, this is easier said than done. It takes quite a gospel imagination and one that is free from the burden of believing that a faithful embodiment of the gospel requires restoring the forms, the alleged pattern, of the churches we read about in the New Testament.

One area where many churches are reluctant to even consider making space for every believer to serve as they are gifted is when it comes to women serving in ministry. Two verses in the New Testament, 1 Corinthians 14:34–35 and 1 Timothy 2:11–12, have loomed large over the discussion of women serving among the church. Here again, space will not allow a detailed look at each passage (there are plenty of commentaries for that), but we do need a more careful reading of each passage and to bring these passages into conversation with the totality of Scripture in light of Jesus Christ and the kingdom of God.

1 Corinthians 14:34–35 reads "women should be silent in the churches. For they are not permitted to speak, but should be subordinate, as the law also says. If there is anything they desire to know, let them ask their husbands at home. For it is shameful for a woman to speak in church." The text is found within a section dealing with matters of the Christian assembly (*ekklēsia*) that begins with 11:2 and runs through the end of chapter 14.

Like the problems throughout 1 Corinthians these assembly matters involve divisions and disruptions which reflect the wisdom of the world rather than the wisdom of Christ-crucified. In chapter 14, the matters at hand involve the gifts of prophecy and tongues, with people of the church interrupting others, as well as some women who are asking disruptive questions. To correct the problem, Paul commands the exercise of silence to those speaking in tongues when there isn't an interpreter (v. 28), to those sharing a word of prophesy when another person has a word to share (v. 30), and to the women (v. 34).

In all three instances, Paul uses the verb *sigaō*, which means to become silent. Paul's concern is ending the "noising confusion" so that the assembly "will glorify God and edify the church."[5] Regarding the women, the intent is not about permanently silencing their voices any more than it is

---

5. Grenz and Kjesbo, *Women in the Church*, 118.

about permanently prohibiting anyone from speaking a word of prophecy or speaking in tongues. For the latter two, Paul is simply issuing an order to stop speaking if there isn't anyone to interpret the word spoken in tongues and so that another person may prophesy.

For the women, Paul's command is more likely issued to some wives rather than all women in general. In the Greek language, the word *anēr* means both man and husband, while the word *gunē* means both woman and wife. Therefore, since the women that Paul was referring to were women with husbands at home, he is speaking about wives becoming silent. His concern is the questions they are asking, which they can ask their husbands at home. It is because of the questions they are asking that Paul is telling the wives to be silent and now speak. Therefore, it is a misuse of this passage to say it addresses and prohibits women from praying and prophesying in the assembly (cf. 1 Cor 11:5) or any form of ministry.

1 Timothy 2:11–12 reads, "Let a woman learn in silence with full submission. I permit no woman to teach or to have authority over a man; she is to keep silent." Like any text, this passage of Scripture has a context that is important to our understanding. The context includes the larger textual location of these verses in the entire second chapter of 1 Timothy as well as the cultural setting of Ephesus, where Timothy is located (1 Tim 1:3), and how that shapes the problems taking place among this church.

There are some Christians who believe the meaning and application of this passage are unequivocally clear. Reading the passage rather literally, it is understood that a woman is neither allowed to teach nor have authority over men. This restriction is based upon the order of creation, in which Adam was created before Eve (v. 13), and therefore these restrictions are universal.[6] Until more recent years, this understanding has, in practice, absolutely restricted women from any leadership in ministry, which included the role of preaching and serving as an elder. In my own Christian tradition, this understanding has historically also excluded women from reading Scripture, offering prayer, and teaching any class whenever there are baptized males present, as well as restricting women from serving vocationally in ministry. Only in recent years has the understandings of

---

6. Douglas J. Moo, "Authority Over Men?," 180. The preface to this book says that the positions of each article are those of the individual authors, yet the editors also state that the conclusions are consistent with the position of the Council on Biblical Manhood and Womanhood. So, when Moo writes, "We think . . ." he is not speaking just for himself but for the editors and presumably the other authors as well as those who hold the position represented here.

some churches changed, shifting to a more gender-inclusive view in which women may serve in ways such as reading Scripture and praying in the presence of men as well as serving in some roles of vocational ministry (e.g., Children's Minister).

A lot of freight seems to be loaded onto this one passage of Scripture and not with any consistency. If we are going to insist that verses 11–12 should be universally and literally applied in every local church, then for the sake of consistency, we should do the same with the other verses in this context of instructions for worship. That is, we ought to insist that only men can lift up holy hands to pray (v. 8), that women should always dress modestly by never wearing any jewelry or braiding their hair (v. 9), and by reminding women that they will be saved through childbearing (v. 15). However, such an approach seems very problematic, which is why such a literal reading of this text seems unfathomable except for the part about women learning in silence and not having any authority over men. When we ponder all the instructions, particularly in verses 8–15, we need to consider the historical circumstances that Timothy was facing. Doing so will help us better understand the text and the implications might be for our own contexts.

This capital city of the province of Asia was known for its worship of Artemis, who was the female goddess of fertility. She represented "the most powerful expression of the Great Mother, who took no second place to a male god."[7] Regarded also as the goddess of childbearing, she sought assistance from a male, and this made her superior to men. Additionally, by the second half of the first century, false teaching known as Gnosticism was emerging among Christianity, which included the church in Ephesus. A part of the Gnostic teaching was that Eve had priority, teaching Adam and thus in a sense giving him life.[8]

Although brief, this historical context provides at least some of the background for the false teaching that Timothy is contending with as he ministers among the church in Ephesus (see 1 Tim 1:18–20, 4:1–8, 5:16, 6:3–10; 2 Tim 2:16–18, 3:1–9, 4:2–4, 14–15). The problem was not that women were to be subordinate to men but that some of the women, influenced by the cultic worship of Artemis and Gnosticism, believed they were superior to men and were acting upon this belief in ways that threatened the church. To correct the problem, Paul issued the instructions we read

---

7. Kroeger, "1 Timothy 2:12," 228.
8. Hicks, *Women Serving God*, 197.

The Spirit-Filled Church

in 1 Timothy 2 not as a universal law but as a corrective measure for the church in Ephesus.

What we find in both v. 9 and v. 15 is a concern that the women of the church assume the proper role that was regarded as proper for their Greco-Roman society.[9] Because Paul uses the words *anēr* (man/husband) and *gunē* (woman/wife), the concern may be with married women and how they are treating their husbands. Nevertheless, these women think they are superior to men, so Paul demands their silence and that they should no longer "teach or assume authority over a man" (NIV), meaning that Paul will no longer allow them "to control" (CEB) these men.[10] This authority or control may even have been a claim to have authorship of men, which explains why Paul mentions the created order of Adam and then Eve (1 Tim 2:13-14).[11] In this sense, Paul does not mention the created order of Adam and Eve as a foundation for the instructions he is giving but as a reminder that, despite what some of these women have believed, women are not the source of men. Furthermore, the well-being of a woman giving birth hinges on the grace of God, which is why the women are instructed to "continue in faith and love, and holiness, with modesty."

When we consider the context, we see that Paul is correcting a problem within the church of Ephesus, not a problem with every church either then or now. Paul is addressing the demeanor in which the women teach and exercise the authority of that role rather than whether women may ever teach.[12] Is there any lesson for contemporary churches in this passage? Of course, there are. Churches everywhere should still pray, including prayers for those elected to political offices. Both men and women should offer prayers from a life set apart for God (holiness) rather than living the selfish kinds of lives that lead to arguments, immodest expressions, and even trying to have one's way by exercising control over others. Those who persist in selfishness and/or are becoming captivated by ideas that are not of the gospel (conspiracy theories?), should not be allowed to teach and that goes for both men and women. But to universalize the particular *how* of Paul's instructions for the church in Ephesus upon churches today imposes a

9. Scholer, "1 Timothy 2:9-15," 197.

10. The word *authenteō* is found nowhere else in the New Testament except in 1 Tim 2:12. Although it is usually translated a "authority," there is some variation in meaning, among which it can mean having control in a dominating manner. See Hubner, "Revisiting αὐθεντέω in 1 Timothy 2:12," 43-44.

11. Kroeger, "1 Timothy 2:12," 231.

12. Hübner, "Revisiting αὐθεντέω in 1 Timothy 2:12," 67.

Part Four: Christ-Formed and Spirit-Filled

corrective response for one context upon different contexts. Doing so also hinders the way the Spirit is gifting some women to serve, limiting how they serve based on problems associated with Artemis and early Gnosticism that seem non existent in churches today.

All Believers Gifted to Serve

As baptized followers of Jesus, we have received the Spirit to live as witnesses of the kingdom of God in the world. We have already noted how, according to Acts 2, the Holy Spirit was poured out on the Day of Pentecost. This was the fulfillment of everything the good news of Jesus Christ and the kingdom of God anticipated, a new community—the church—living in the name of Jesus and by the power of the Holy Spirit.

The citation of the prophet Joel by Peter in Acts 2 begins with these words, "In the last days . . ." (v. 17). In the great span of history, the final age has begun. God has raised the crucified Jesus from death and exalted him as Lord. So, God has already won the great cosmic battle. Even though the full realization of this victory awaits the second coming of Jesus, the outcome has now become manifest.

This is why the apostle Paul speaks of Christians as a new creation in Christ. 2 Corinthians 5:17 says, "So if anyone is in Christ, there is a new creation: everything old has passed away; see, everything has become new." In other words, the church is the future, new creation in Christ, dwelling in the present among the old creation. This is the proleptic reality of the church and therefore the reality which the church, both universal and local, must embody.

As the new creation of God, the Pentecost sermon of Acts 2 is clear that the vision of new creation includes the outpouring of the Spirit upon all flesh—that is, upon both male and female, both young and old. This outpouring of the Spirit is the sign of God's salvation upon every one that calls upon the name of Jesus. So, for both men and women, serving as the Spirit has gifted them, whether that is feeding the hungry, encouraging the bereaved, or preaching the word of God, is a signpost of the new creation God has fulfilled in Christ. Therefore, whatever claims we believe the sin of Adam and Eve makes about the roles men and women have in the fallen world, the life of the church is to be formed as new creation rather than the old creation.[13]

13. McKnight, *The Blue Parakeet*, 189., "Christian men and women are to live a life

The Spirit-Filled Church

Because God has poured his Spirit out upon all of his new creation, the church is the formation of a life where all is held in common. There are not any believers favored over others; rather, all believers participate in a life that we may describe as egalitarian. That is, as the word *egalitarianism* implies, all believers are equal. This is why, at the end of Acts 2, we read a description of life in which the believers generously share their goods with each other and eat together as well as pray and attend to the teaching of the apostles together (vs. 42–47).

This egalitarian formation as new creation was not always so easily embodied though. Sometimes there were problems within different churches that needed correction, as we've already seen in both 1 Corinthians and 1 Timothy. Sometimes, though, the problem was that certain believers thought a marker, other than their baptism, identified them as Christian and therefore having status before God. This was the problem with the Galatians, where some Jewish believers thought that in addition to faith in Christ, the Law of Moses identified them as God's people. For Paul, that was a rejection of the gospel, and he would not have any of that. All who had received baptism into Christ now equally belonged to Christ. As Paul writes, "There is no longer Jew or Greek, there is no longer slave or free, there is no longer male or female; for all of you are one in Christ Jesus" (Gal 3:28).

Whatever previous status that marked people among old creation, their baptism into Christ marks them as a new creation and therefore gives them a new status as equals in Christ. This is more than just sharing equally in the blessings of salvation like the forgiveness of sins and having the promise of eternal life. Ethnicity and gender, as well as slave or free, were all social statuses too, and it is these social statuses that are equalized in Christ because those who are in Christ belong to the new creation. Because this is God's act of redemption, old creation is transformed and made new out of all that was fallen among the old.[14] This new life is formed by the Spirit who is not bound by the categories of the old creation but instead gifts all, including men and women, to serve as they are gifted for life as God's new creation in Christ.

---

that moves beyond the fall, beyond the battle of wills. If new creation does anything, it unleashes the power to undo the fall in our world. I cannot emphasize this enough: the story of the Bible is the story of new creation in Christ. The words of Genesis 3:16, to put the matter directly, are overcome in new creation."

14. Hicks, *Women Serving God*, 115.

Part Four: Christ-Formed and Spirit-Filled

This eschatological vision in which the church is the proleptic embodiment of the gospel that is and is to come offers a new lens through which we read the New Testament. That includes our reading of who may serve in what capacity, including women. The Spirit is poured out upon all believers but gifts different believers with different gifts so that together the church may fully embody the gospel. So, rather than deciding who can serve in what capacity through the lens of a few verses meant to correct problems within some of the early churches, we ought to make such decisions based upon this eschatological vision that includes the outpouring of the Spirit upon all. That is, the local church should ordain people to serve as the Spirit has gifted them. This includes ordaining women who have received the gift of preaching and teaching and/or pastoring to serve as ministers preaching the gospel and/or shepherds caring for the souls of the church.

The first woman I ever heard preach was Barbara Brown Taylor. I've heard very few women from my own church tradition preach since the Churches of Christ still mostly restrict women from preaching, but I've had the opportunity to hear Sarah Barton and Tiffany Dahlman preach before. Like Barbara Brown Taylor, their sermons were preached with passion and called the church into the way of Jesus according to the particular passage of Scripture they preached from. It was clear to my eyes and ears, as well as the eyes and ears of the congregation, which happened to be those gathered for *Harbor: The Pepperdine Bible Lectures*, that the Spirit had gifted them to preach the word of God. At the time, I was still uneasy with the idea of a woman preaching because it was so different from my own experience. I no longer believed that God, according to Scripture, forever excluded women from preaching, but recognizing that on an intellectual level and accepting it in practice was a different manner. Similar to the apostle Peter in relation to Cornelius, I had to recognize that God is impartial with both the gift of salvation and with the giving of the gift of preaching. It was clear that the Spirit had anointed these women to preach the word of God, and so I could no longer withhold that ministry from them since their gift of preaching was from the Spirit of God. *Selah*.

Conclusion

One of our contemporary American prophets, Bob Dylan, sang a song called "The Times They Are a-Changin."

Come gather 'round people, where you roam,

The Spirit-Filled Church

and admit that the waters around you have grown . . .
For the times, they are a-changin'.

Though the song is nearly sixty years old, it seems as relevant today as when first released in 1964. Change is taking place around every corner, and most corners seem to appear before we're ready to navigate the next turn.

Undoubtedly, our ever-changing culture comes with many challenges for leading churches to live on mission with God. Still, we press on believing that the churches we serve among are called to follow Jesus within their local contexts as an embodied gospel. This hardly answers all the questions of what such a life will look like. Some of these questions can only be answered through a process of discernment as a local church listening to Scripture, tradition, and culture. However, we are not left just shooting in the wind with a chance that we might hit a target. Far from such randomness, the Spirit of God dwells among every believer and so among the church.

The Holy Spirit is sent by God to the church but neither for arbitrary nor capricious endeavors. Rather, the Spirit forms our life to reflect the very essence of God revealed in Jesus. In doing so, the Spirit endows every believer with different gifts and talents to serve as a contributor to the church's participation in the mission of God. Part of discovering how our local churches are called to embody the gospel in a contextualized manner begins by taking inventory of how the Spirit has gifted the different believers among the church. As we recognize the way the Spirit is empowering both men and women to serve, whether such service might be managing a food distribution for those in need or preaching, we submit to the work of the Spirit. Because such submission is faithfulness to Jesus, we can trust that God will bring about his redemptive good in his time. When problems, such as distortions of the gospel or behaviors that undermine the integrity of the gospel, we may discern the need to take some corrective measures that would, at least for a time, limit how certain people exercise their spiritual gifts. However, this should be the exception rather than the norm. In the absence of any such problems, we should recognize and encourage every believer to serve as the Spirit of God has anointed them so that the church may serve together as followers of Jesus. This is how the church continues participating in the mission of God as a faithful but contextual embodiment of the gospel.

Conclusion

Think Local, but What If . . .

As I write, we are now going on two years and counting. That's the time that has passed since COVID-19 became a pandemic. Every facet of society has been impacted by this novel coronavirus, and that includes the life of local churches. The challenges have been significant. So, whatever we think about online worship gatherings, hangouts on Zoom, and so forth, they were responses that churches made in good faith rather than just throwing in the towel when life became difficult.

Many local churches seem to have weathered the storm, so to speak, but even as society is slowly recovering from the crisis presented by COVID-19, there are still challenges facing churches. Still called to live as participants in the mission of God, local churches face the question of what our participation in the mission of God might look like going forward. Last year I preached a sermon to the Newark Church of Christ that I called *Post COVID-19 and Going Forward.* In that message, I described our church with the metaphor of a ship wisely harboring in the port for the safety of everyone.

This metaphor of a ship harboring safely in the port seems true of a lot of local churches, and as mentioned, I think it was the wise response. I don't know any church that particularly enjoyed canceling church services and going online. That's also true for many of the other necessary social-distancing practices, but such decisions were wise and a way of loving our neighbors. With that said, a ship cannot remain in the harbor forever.

Conclusion

As John A. Shedd once said, "A ship in the harbor is safe, but that is not what ships are built for." And so, churches must begin to sail again, but there are some questions to ask. If we think of the local church as a ship, then we must ask about the direction God wants these ships to sail in. What should our churches continue doing, and what might our churches need to discontinue? Essentially, we might ask *what needs to happen going forward so that our churches continue participating in the mission of God?*

Such questions call for discernment because the answers are unlikely to be easy. Going forward means going where we haven't gone. Although doing so will involve many of the practices we have learned along the journey thus far, we will also need to let go of some habits as we learn new ways. In doing so, we continue stepping forward as participants in the mission of God in ways that remain faithful, and thus a coherent embodiment of the gospel while also contextualizing, and thus translating, the gospel we proclaim. I hope the book you have now read has communicated this point about participation in the mission of God clearly as well as given a hermeneutical framework for such participation as people who take the Bible seriously. Yet it is one thing to talk about such participation and another thing to actually do. The latter is more challenging, and that means it is easier for churches to retreat into the "familiar and comfortable" harbor than to press forward. So, let me share a bit more of that message I shared with my church, a lesson we learn from Israel (and a lesson I am indebted to my friend Fred Liggin for helping me see).

We pick up the story of Israel as they are wandering in the wilderness. Israel had suffered oppression as slaves in Egypt for four hundred thirty years (Exod 12:40–41) when God called Moses to lead them out of Egypt and into the promised land of Canaan. However, the journey from Egypt to Canaan was far from easy. Pharaoh did not want to let the Israelites go, and so the first fourteen chapters of Exodus tell of this epic battle between the Lord and Pharaoh. Of course, the Lord won, and Israel was set free from their captivity in Egypt, but that was not the end of the challenge in getting to the promised land. Besides the challenges from Pharaoh, there were challenges from the stubbornness of Israel and the effect which their resistance had on their journey into the promised land.

The journey from Horeb in Egypt to Kadesh Barnea at the edge of the promised land was eleven days (Deut 1:2), but it took Israel forty years to make this journey. Why? Well, the answer is found in the book of Numbers.

Conclusion

In chapter 13 of Numbers, we read how Moses had sent out men to explore the territory and they returned after forty days. Having observed some strong people living in the land, the men were afraid and insisted that Israel could not go up against these people. This report caused great anxiety among Israel, and as a leader knows, anxiety becomes a real threat to accomplishing the vision. In fact, when people become anxious, they will not only attempt to sabotage whatever plans are in place, but they will even attempt to come to illogical decisions that only cause harm. This was the case for Israel too, as we read in Numbers 14:1–4:

> Then all the congregation raised a loud cry, and the people wept that night. And all the Israelites complained against Moses and Aaron; the whole congregation said to them, "Would that we had died in the land of Egypt! Or would that we had died in this wilderness! Why is the Lord bringing us into this land to fall by the sword? Our wives and our little ones will become booty; would it not be better for us to go back to Egypt?" So they said to one another, "Let us choose a captain, and go back to Egypt."

For all the brutality that Israel suffered in Egypt, their anxiety over the difficulty that is ahead of them has them attempting to sabotage the plans for entering the promised land. Instead of continuing forward, the Israelites are now wishing they would have either died or could just go back to Egypt. Even worse, their anxiety has them wishing they could replace Moses rather than listening to him and allowing him to lead. Israel now wants someone who will lead them according to their own anxiety-fueled desires (this might explain a lot about why many churches, especially among autonomous non-denominational churches, so easily fire their pastors).

Now, Israel has come to a point in their journey where the difficulties ahead of them mean that rather than continuing to participate in the mission of God, they are choosing disobedience to the Lord. As a result, the Lord instructed Moses to say to the Israelites, "According to the number of the days in which you spied out the land, forty days, for every day a year, you shall bear your iniquity, forty years, and you shall know my displeasure" (Num 14:34). This anxiety-fueled disobedience on the part of Israel is the reason an eleven-day journey from Egypt into the promised land became a forty-year journey. What was, understandably, a challenging journey became much more difficult all because Israel allowed the concern for safety and avoiding the challenges ahead to become their masters.

Conclusion

I'm sharing this segment of Israel's story because I understand the challenges that churches are facing. Stepping forward on mission with God will not be easy, and the onset of the COVID-19 pandemic has only increased the challenges. Furthermore, change is always difficult, especially for churches with rich traditions. Some Christians don't want change, while others find such change extremely stressful. A few Christians, perhaps, just don't understand the need for change and don't seem willing to even try. All of this creates anxiety, and when such anxiety arises, it's tempting to go back to the way things were because that's easier.

Stepping forward on mission with God is hard. But we really have to ask if going back to the way we did church before COVID-19 is what God really wants. Could it be that God is trying to lead us forward? Could it be that God is using this great disruption of the pandemic to lead churches into some new ways of faithfully embodying the gospel? I believe so, but that leaves us with the question of how. Or, as we asked earlier, *what needs to happen going forward so that our churches continue participating in the mission of God?*

For the most part, I have avoided answering any specific answers as to what it might look like for a local church to participate in the mission of God. That is because I believe those specific answers are best answered by the local churches as they attend to the scriptures, tradition, and cultural context of their local communities. This is part of the reason I titled this conclusion *Think Local, but What If* . . . As we discern the necessity in our churches, we make those changes with courage, conviction, and wisdom. The impact is that our churches discover new ways of faithfully but contextually participating in the mission of God. Yet sometimes those changes reach beyond our local context.

In the last few years, our church has increasingly started using the *Discovery Bible Study* (DBS) method in our campus ministry. This is a method that relies on people just reading the Bible and answering open questions about what the story in Scripture teaches us about God, ourselves, and what sort of practices Scripture calls us to put into practice. The genius of this approach is that anyone can facilitate a Bible study, as it does not depend on an "expert" or a study guide, and that it is reproducible. That is, as people learn to follow Jesus, they can invite others to read the Bible with them and use the questions to facilitate the Bible study.

Well, I received an email sharing how a supporter of our campus ministry learned about our using the DBS method, and they began using that

Conclusion

method. They are now reading the Bible with about forty men and women from Afghanistan who have never read the Bible before. What a reminder that even though our participation in the mission of God always begins with the way we serve locally as churches, the impact can reach far beyond our local communities. That's because God is working throughout the entire world, and my hope is that this book you have now finished will help us all more faithfully join in the work God is doing.

Bibliography

Allen, Leonard. *Poured Out: The Spirit of God Empowering the Mission of God*. Abilene: ACU Press, 2018.

Aristides. *The Apology of Aristides the Philosopher*. 15. Early Christian Writings. http://www.earlychristianwritings.com/text/aristides-kay.html.

Arterburn, Stephen, and Dean Merrill, eds. *Every Man's Bible NIV*, Deluxe ed. Carol Stream, IL: Tyndale House Publishers, 2015. Available at https://www.barnesandnoble.com/w/every-mans-bible-nlt-stephen-arterburn/1119362862?ean=9781414381077#/.

Bartholomew, Craig G., and Michael W. Goheen. *The Drama of Scripture: Finding Our Place in the Biblical Story*. Grand Rapids, MI: Baker Academic, 2004.

Barton, Ruth Haley. *Pursuing God's Will Together: A Discernment Practice for Leadership Groups*. Downers Grove: InterVarsity, 2012.

Bates, Matthew W. *Salvation by Allegiance Alone: Rethinking Faith, Works, and the Gospel of Jesus the King*. Grand Rapids: Baker Academic, 2017.

Bauckham, Richard. *Bible and Mission: Christian Witness in a Postmodern World*. Grand Rapids: Baker Academic, 2003.

Beale, G.K., and Mitchell Kim. *God Dwells Among Us: Expanding Eden to the Ends of the Earth*. Downers Grove: InterVarsity, 2014.

Blake, Aaron. "Kellyanne Conway says Donald Trump's team has 'alternative facts.' Which pretty much says it all." *The Washington Post*. January 22, 2017. https://www.washingtonpost.com/news/the-fix/wp/2017/01/22/kellyanne-conway-says-donald-trumps-team-has-alternate-facts-which-pretty-much-says-it-all/.

Bonhoeffer, Dietrich. *The Cost of Discipleship*. New York: Macmillan, 1959. Reprint, New York: Touchtone, 1995.

———. *Discipleship*. Dietrich Bonhoeffer Works, vol 4., edited by Geoffrey B. Kelly, and John D. Godsey. Minneapolis, MN: Fortress, 2003.

Bosch, David J. *Transforming Mission: Paradigm Shifts in Theology of Mission*. Maryknoll, NY: Orbis, 1991.

Bibliography

Breen, Mike, and Steve Cockram, *Building a Discipling Culture: How to Release a Missional Movement by Discipling People Like Jesus Did*. Pawleys Island, SC: 3 Dimension Ministries, 2011.

Bruce, F.F. *The Gospel of John: Introduction, Exposition, and Notes*. Grand Rapids: Eerdmans, 1983.

Brueggemann, Walter. *Theology of the Old Testament: Testimony, Dispute, Advocacy*. Minneapolis: Fortress, 1997.

Byrne, Brendan. *A Costly Freedom: A Theological Reading of Mark's Gospel*. Collegeville, MN: The Liturgical, 2008.

Camp, Lee C. *Mere Discipleship: Radical Christianity in a Rebellious World*. Grand Rapids: Brazos, 2003.

———. *Scandalous Witness: A Little Political Manifesto for Christians*. Grand Rapids: Eerdmans, 2020.

Campbell, Alexander. *The Christian System: In Reference to the Union of Christians and a Restoration of Primitive Christianity, As Plead in the Current Reformation*. Cincinnati: Bosworth, Chase, and Hall Publishers, 1835. https://archive.org/details/christiansystemoocamp.

Campbell, Thomas. *Declaration and Address of the Christian Association of Washington*. 1809. https://webfiles.acu.edu/departments/Library/HR/restmov_nov11/www.mun.ca/rels/restmov/texts/tcampbell/da/DA-1ST.HTM.

Chan, Francis. *Multiply: Disciples Making Disciples*. Colorado Springs, CO: David C. Cook, 2012.

Charry, Ellen T. *By the Renewing of Your Minds: The Pastoral Function of Christian Doctrine*. New York: Oxford University Press, 1997.

Chiu, Allyson. "'They are worthy of death': A cop preached that the government should execute LGBTQ people." *The Washington Post*. June 14, 2019. https://www.washingtonpost.com/nation/2019/06/14/they-are-worthy-death-cop-preached-that-government-should-execute-lgbtq-people/?utm_term=.44716e17a0ef (Accessed July 8, 2019).

Clement, *First Clement*. Edited and Translated by Cyril C. Richardson. *Early Christian Fathers*. New York: Touchtone, 1996.

Clément, Olivier. *The Roots of Christian Mysticism: Texts from the Patristic Era with Commentary*, 2nd ed. Hyde Park: New City, 1993.

Donahue, Bill, and Russ Robinson. *Building a Church of Small Groups: A Place Where Nobody Stands Alone*. Grand Rapids: Zondervan, 2001.

Donavan, Vincent J. *Christianity Rediscovered: Twenty-Fifth Anniversary Edition*. Maryknoll, NY: Orbis, 2003.

Dostoevsky, Fyodor. *The Brothers Karamazov*. Translated by Richard Pevear, and Larissa Volokhonsky. New York: Everyman's Library, 1992.

Dunn, James D.G. *The Theology of Paul the Apostle*. Grand Rapids: Eerdmans, 1998.

Edwards, David. "Georgia councilman says interracial marriage is 'just not the way a Christian is supposed to live.'" *Raw Story*. May 6, 2019. https://www.rawstory.com/2019/05/georgia-councilman-says-interracial-marriage-is-just-not-the-way-a-christian-is-supposed-to-live/.

Fitch, David E. *Faithful Presence: Seven Disciplines That Shape the Church for Mission*. Downers Grove: IVP, 2016.

———. *The Great Giveaway: Reclaiming the Mission of the Church From Big Business, Parachurch Organizations, Psychotherapy, Consumer Capitalism, and Other Modern Maladies*. Grand Rapids: Baker, 2005.

Bibliography

Frei, Hans. *The Eclipse of Biblical Narrative: A Study in Eighteenth and Nineteenth Century Hermeneutics.* New Haven, CT: Yale University Press, 1974.

Frost, Michael, and Alan Hirsch. *The Shaping of Things to Come: Innovation and Mission for the 21st-Century Church*, rev. ed. Grand Rapids, MI: Baker, 2013.

———. *ReJesus: A Wild Messiah for a Missional Church.* Peabody, MA: Hendrickson, 2009.

Gorman, Michael. *Becoming the Gospel: Paul, Participation, and Mission.* Grand Rapids: Eerdmans, 2015.

———. *Cruciformity: Paul's Narrative Spirituality of the Cross.* Grand Rapids: Eerdmans, 2001.

———. *Inhabiting the Cruciform God: Kenosis, Justification, and Theosis in Paul's Narrative Soteriology.* Grand Rapids, MI: Eerdmans, 2009.

Grenz, Stanley J., and John Franke. *Beyond Foundationalism: Shaping Theology in a Postmodern Context.* Louisville: Westminster John Knox, 2001.

Grenz, Stanley J., and Denise Muir Kjesbo. *Women in the Church: A Biblical Theology of Women in Ministry.* Downers Grove: InterVarsity, 1995.

Grenz, Stanley J. *Created for Community: Connecting Christian Belief with Christian Living.* Grand Rapids: BridgePoint, 1996.

———. *Theology for the Community of God.* Grand Rapids: Eerdmans, 1994.

Guder, Darrell L., et al. *Missional Church: A Vision for the Sending of the Church in North America.* Grand Rapids: Eerdmans, 1998.

Halík, Tomáš. *Night of the Confessor: Christian Faith in an Age of Uncertainty.* Translated by Gerald Turner. New York: Image, 2012.

Hall, Douglas John. *The End of Christendom and the Future of Christianity.* Eugene, OR: Wipf and Stock, 1997.

Hart, David Bentley. *The Beauty and the Infinite: The Aesthetics of Christian Truth.* Grand Rapids: Eerdmans, 2003.

Hayford, Jack, ed. *NKJV Spirit-Filled Life Bible*, 3rd ed. Nashville, TN Thomas Nelson, 2018. https://www.barnesandnoble.com/w/nkjv-spirit-filled-life-bible-third-edition-hardcover-red-letter-edition-comfort-print-thomas-nelson/1127480991?ean=9780529100146#/.

Hays, Richard B. *The Moral Vision of the New Testament: Community, Cross, and New Creation; A Contemporary Introduction to New Testament Ethics.* New York: HarperCollins, 1996.

Hicks, John Mark. *Searching for the Pattern: My Journey in Interpreting the Bible*, 2019.

———. *Women Serving God: My Journey in Understanding Their Story in the Bible.* Nashville: John Mark Hicks, 2020.

Hiebert, D. Edmond. "God's Creative Masterpiece." *Direction* 23 (Spring 1994) 116–24.

Highfield, Ron. *God, Freedom, & Human Dignity: Embracing a God-Centered Identity in a Me-Centered Culture.* Downers Grove: IVP, 2013.

Hübner, Jamin. "Revisiting αὐθεντέω in 1 Timothy 2:12: What Do the Extant Data Really Show?" *Journal for the Study of Paul and his Letters*, 5, No. 1 (Summer 2015) 41–70.

Hughes, Richard T. *Reviving the Ancient Faith: The Story of Churches of Christ in America.* Grand Rapids: Eerdmans, 1996.

Hunter III, George G. *Church for the Unchurched.* Nashville: Abingdon, 1996.

———. *How to Reach Secular People.* Nashville: Abingdon, 1992.

Ince Jr., Irwin L. *The Beautiful Community: Unity, Diversity, and the Church at Its Best.* Downers Grove: InterVarsity, 2020.

Bibliography

Itkowitz, Colby. "Her son shot their daughters 10 years ago. Then, these Amish families embraced her as a friend." *The Washington Post* (October 1, 2016). https://www.washingtonpost.com/news/inspired-life/wp/2016/10/01/10-years-ago-her-son-killed-amish-children-their-families-immediately-accepted-her-into-their-lives/.

Jacobs, Alan. *How to Think: A Survival Guide for a World at Odds*. New York: Currency, 2017.

Johnson, Luke Timothy. *The Acts of the Apostles*. Sacra Pagina. Collegeville, MN: The Liturgical, 1992.

Joyner, Chris. "Georgia mayor under fire for alleged remarks about black job candidate." *Atlanta Journal Constitution*. May 6, 2019. https://www.ajc.com/news/local-govt—politics/georgia-mayor-under-fire-for-alleged-remarks-about-black-job-candidate/Qr4o3ZLnF5VuB8CzpngLjP/.

Kant, Immanuel. *The Metaphysics of Ethics*, 3rd. ed. Translated by J.W. Semple. Edinburgh: T & T Clark, 1886. http://oll.libertyfund.org/titles/kant-the-metaphysics-of-ethics.

King Jr., Martin Luther. "Letter From Birmingham City Jail." *A Testament of Hope: The Essential Writings and Speeches*. Edited by James M. Washington. New York: HarperCollins, 1986; reprint ed., 2003, 290.

Kinnaman, David and Gabe Lyons. *Unchristian: What a New Generation Really Thinks About Christianity . . . and Why It Matters*. Grand Rapids: Baker, 2007.

Kroeger, Catherine Clark. "1 Timothy 2:12—A Classicist's View." In *Women, Authority, and the Bible*, edited by Alvera Mickelsen. Downers Grove: InterVarsity, 1986.

Kuhn, Thomas S. *The Structure of Scientific Revolutions*. Chicago: The University of Chicago Press, 1962; 3rd ed., 1996, 52.

Ladd, George Eldon. *A Theology of the New Testament*, Rev. ed., edited by Donald A. Hagner. Grand Rapids: Eerdmans, 1993.

Lee, Richard G., ed. *The American Patriot's Bible*. Nashville, TN: Thomas Nelson, 2009. https://www.barnesandnoble.com/w/american-patriots-bible-thomas-nelson/1102088022?ean=9781418541538#/ (Accessed on July 10, 2019).

Letter to Diognetus. Edited and Translated by Cyril C. Richardson. *Early Christian Fathers*. New York: Touchstone, 1996.

Lindbeck, George A. *The Nature of Doctrine: Religion and Theology in a Postliberal Age*. Louisville: Westminster John Knox, 1984.

Lipscomb, David. "The Cholera and the Christian Religion." *Gospel Advocate* 15.28 (July 17, 1873) 649–53.

MacIntyre, Alasdair. *After Virtue: A Study in Moral Theory*, 3rd ed. Notre Dame: University of Notre Dame Press, 2007.

McDonald, Lee Martin. *The Biblical Canon: Its Origin, Transmission, and Authority*. Grand Rapids: Baker Academic, 2007.

McKnight, Scot. *The Blue Parakeet: Rethinking How You Read the Bible*, 2nd ed. Grand Rapids: Zondervan, 2018.

———. *The King Jesus Gospel: The Original Good News Revisited*. Grand Rapids: Zondervan, 2011.

———. *The Kingdom Conspiracy: Returning to the Radical Mission of the Local Church*. Grand Rapids: Brazos, 2014.

———. *One Life: Jesus Calls, We Follow*. Grand Rapids, MI: Zondervan, 2010.

———. *Pastor Paul: Nurturing a Culture of Christoformity in the Church*. Theological Explorations for the Church. Grand Rapids: Brazos, 2019.

———. *Reading Romans Backwards: A Gospel of Peace in the Midst of Empire*. Waco: Baylor University Press, 2019.

Bibliography

Mills, C. Wright. *The Sociological Imagination: Fortieth Anniversary Edition*. New York: Oxford, 1959, 2000.

Mittelberg, Mark. *Building a Contagious Church: Revolutionizing the Way We View and Do Evangelism*. Grand Rapids: Zondervan, 2000.

Moltmann, Jürgen. *The Church in the Power of the Spirit: A Contribution to Messianic Ecclesiology*. Translated by Margaret Kohl. New York: Harper & Row, 1977. Reprint, Minneapolis: Fortress, 1993.

———. *Theology of Hope: On the Grounds and Implications of a Christian Eschatology*. Translated by Margaret Kohl. New York: Harper & Row, 1967. Reprint, Minneapolis: Fortress, 1993.

Moo, Douglas J. "What Does It Mean Not to Teach or Have Authority Over Men?: 1 Timothy 2:11–15." In *Recovering Biblical Manhood and Womanhood: A Response to Evangelical Feminism*, edited by John Piper and Wayne Grudem. Wheaton: Crossway, 1991.

Newbigin, Lesslie. *The Open Secret: An Introduction to the Theology of Mission*, Rev. ed. Grand Rapids: Eerdmans, 1995.

Olbricht, Thomas H. "Hermeneutics in the Churches of Christ." *Restoration Quarterly* 37 (Jan 1995) 1–24.

Osborn, Ronal E. *Death Before the Fall: Biblical Literalism and the Problem of Animal Suffering*. Downers Grove: InterVarsity, 2014.

Palmer, Sean. *Unarmed Empire: In Search of a Beloved Community*. Eugene, OR: Cascade, 2017.

Peace, Richard V. *Conversion in the New Testament: Paul and the Twelve*. Grand Rapids, MI: Eerdmans, 1999.

Pennington, Jonathan T. *The Sermon on the Mount and Human Flourishing: A Theological Commentary*. Grand Rapids: Baker Academic, 2017.

Placher, William C. "Hans Frei and the Meaning of Biblical Narrative." *The Christian Century* 106 (May 1989) 556–59.

Platt, David. *Radical: Taking Back Your Faith From the American Dream*. Colorado Springs, CO: Multnomah, 2010.

Polycarp. *To the Philippians*. Edited and Translated by Cyril C. Richardson. *Early Christian Fathers*. New York: Touchtone, 1996.

Powell, Mark E., John Mark Hicks, and Greg McKinzie. *Discipleship in Community: A Theological Vision for the Future*. Abilene: ACU Press, 2020.

Sarna, Nahum M. "Genesis: The Traditional Hebrew Text with the New JPS Translation." In *The JPS Torah Commentary*, vol. 1. Philadelphia: The Jewish Publication Society, 1989.

Scholer, David M. "1 Timothy 2:9–15 and The Place of Women in the Church's Ministry." In *Women, Authority, and the Bible*, edited by Alvera Mickelsen. Downers Grove: InterVarsity, 1986.

Schreiner, Thomas S. *Paul: Apostle of God's Glory in Christ*. Downers Grove: InterVarsity, 2001.

Sedmak, Clemens. *Doing Local Theology: A Guide for Artisans of a New Humanity*. Maryknoll, NY: Orbis, 2002.

Sider, Ronald J. *The Scandal of the Evangelical Conscience: Why Are Christians Living Just Like the Rest of the World?* Grand Rapids: Baker, 2005.

Silva, Moisés. *Philippians*. Baker Exegetical Commentary on the New Testament, 2 ed. Grand Rapids: Baker Academic, 2005.

Bibliography

Sittser, Gerald L. *Water from a Deep Well: Christian Spirituality from Early Martyrs to Modern Missionaries*. Downers Grove: InterVarsity, 2007.

Smith, Christian. *The Bible Made Impossible: Why Biblicism Is Not a Truly Evangelical Reading of Scripture*. Grand Rapids: Brazos, 2011.

Stetzer, Ed, and Mike Dodson. *Comeback Churches: How 300 Churches Turned Around and Yours Can Too*. Nashville: Broadman and Holman, 2007.

Stetzer, Ed, and David Putman. *Breaking The Missional Code: Your Church Can Become a Missionary in Your Community*. Nashville: Broadman and Holman, 2006.

Stone, Bryan. *Evangelism after Christendom: The Theology and Practice of Christian Witness*. Grand Rapids: Brazos, 2007.

Stott, John R.W. "The Message of the Sermon on the Mount." In *The Bible Speaks Today*. Downers Grove: InterVarsity, 1978.

Taylor, Charles. *A Secular Age*. Cambridge: The Belknap Press of Harvard University Press, 2007.

Toulmin, Steven. *Cosmopolis: The Hidden Agenda of Modernity*. Chicago: The University of Chicago Press, 1990.

Vanhoozer, Kevin J. *Faith Speaking Understanding: Performing the Drama of Doctrine*. Louisville: Westminster John Knox, 2014.

Volf, Miroslav. *Captive to the Word of God: Engaging the Scriptures for Contemporary Theological Reflection*. Grand Rapids: Eerdmans, 2010.

Von Balthasar, Hans Urs. *Engagement With God*. Translated by R. John Halliburton. Einsiedeln: Johannes Verlag, 1971. San Francisco: Ignatius, 2008.

Vreeland, Derek. *By the Way: Getting Serious About Following Jesus*. Harrisonburg, VA: Herald, 2019.

Walton, John H. *The Lost World of Adam and Eve: Genesis 2–3 and the Human Origins Debate*. Downers Grove: InterVarsity, 2015.

———. *The Lost World of Genesis One: Ancient Cosmology and the Origins Debate*. Downers Grove: InterVarsity, 2009.

Warren, Rick. *The Purpose Driven Church: Growth Without Compromising Your Message and Mission*. Grand Rapids: Zondervan, 1995.

Willard, Dallas. *The Divine Conspiracy: Rediscovering Our Hidden Life in God*. New York: HarperCollins, 1997.

———. *Renovation of the Heart: Putting on the Character of Christ*, 2nd ed. Colorado Springs: Navpress, 2012.

Wright, Christopher J.H. *The Mission of God: Unlocking the Bible's Grand Narrative*. Downers Grove: IVP Academic, 2006.

Wright, N.T. *Justification: God's Plan and Paul's Vision*. Downers Grove: IVP Academic, 2009.

———. *The New Testament and the People of God*. Christian Origins and the Question of God, vol. 1. Minneapolis: Fortress, 1992.

———. *Paul and the Faithfulness of God: Book II, Parts III and IV*. Christian Origins and the Question of God, vol. 4. Minneapolis: Fortress, 2013.

———. *Scripture and the Authority of God: How to Read the Bible Today*. New York: HarperCollins, 2011.

www.ingramcontent.com/pod-product-compliance
Lightning Source LLC
Chambersburg PA
CBHW062003180426
43198CB00036B/2165